Words That Move Mountains

ANDY OWEN

Words That Move Mountains

First Edition (2024)

Copyright © 2024 Andy Owen
All rights reserved.

ISBN: 9798324435974

Published by Andy Owen Copy & Creative Ltd

www.andyowencopyandcreative.com

"Writing a book is a horrible, exhausting struggle, like a long bout with some painful illness. One would never undertake such a thing, if one were not driven on by some demon whom one can neither resist nor understand." **George Orwell**

This is not just a book. It is your personal conversation with the greatest minds in communication, creativity and life.

You will be inspired, moved and influenced on <u>every single page</u>, with advice and guidance from the world's most iconic industry and global figures, brought together - for the very first time - in this book.

They are giants, every one of them.

From the golden quill of David Ogilvy to the visionary insights of Twain, Wilde, Lennon and Hemingway - and the inspirational leadership of Churchill, Lincoln and so many other inspirational people - this book, 'Words That Move Mountains' is your personal encyclopaedia of astonishing wisdom.

It is timeless advice and guidance that has inspired so many - and set standards, built brands, forged empires - and transformed marketplaces everywhere. On the pages of 'Words That Move Mountains' you will discover:

Copy and Communication Secrets *that sold millions.* **Creative Strategies** *that outlived their creators.* **Inspirational Wisdom** *that continues to motivate leaders, decision makers and innovators around the globe.*

This book is your opportunity to see further, by standing on the mighty shoulders of titans. The profound insights and genius inspiration within this book, will redefine the way you think about communication, creativity and success.

You'll find yourself returning to its timeless wisdom again and again, to be stirred, uplifted, and propelled forever onwards and upwards.

'Words That Move Mountains' *isn't just a great read. It's much more than that. It's a journey - a wonderful odyssey of the mind and spirit - that will leave you continually inspired and forever changed.*

Enjoy…

Andy Owen

Brea Village, Cornwall,

England

May 2024

Table of Contents

Introduction 1

Section 1 – Advice and Inspiration 4

Persistence and Resilience 5

Customer Focus and Marketing 10

Creativity and Originality 16

Leadership, Success and Failure 20

Personal Development and Growth 24

Business and Strategy 30

Life, Philosophy, Wisdom and Knowledge 34

Humour and Perspective 40

Critical Views and Commentary 46

Inspirational and Motivational 53

Section 2 - Creative 59

The Essence of Creativity 60

Creativity vs. Effectiveness 63

The Creative Process 66

Challenges to Creativity 68

Creativity and the Consumer 71

Creativity and Innovation in Advertising 74

Creativity Under Scrutiny 76

Personal Insights on Creativity 79

Section 3 - Copy 82

The Writing Process 84

Understanding Your Audience 90

Crafting Compelling Messages 94

Creativity and Originality 99

Headlines and Attention-Grabbing Techniques 101
Persuasion and Emotional Appeal 106
Clarity and Simplicity 108
Testing and Optimisation 112
Inspirational and Motivational 115
Ethics and Authenticity 118

ABOUT YOUR AUTHOR 124

Introduction

Your inspirational journey begins…

Welcome, dear reader, to an inspirational journey through the realms of wisdom, creativity - and the unparalleled power of words.

It's a beacon for those who dare to dream, create - and inspire.

Within these pages, lies a treasure trove of inspiration from the most brilliant minds in industry and history.

Each quote will ignite a spark within you - to challenge the boundaries of what you believed was possible - and to guide you towards achieving greatness beyond your wildest dreams.

Firstly, we step into the realm of **ADVICE & INSPIRATION**.

This section is the cornerstone of our collective journey, offering pearls of wisdom that educate, motivate and illuminate the path forward.

These quotes are more than just words, they are life lessons. Advice and guidance from the past, influencing calls to action for the future.

They are here to remind you that the journey to greatness is both an ongoing challenge and a celebration, fraught with obstacles but rich with rewards.

We then transition into the **CREATIVE** world.

This is where structure meets imagination, where proven layouts and innovative approaches, converge to elevate your message to a level you never thought possible.

It's a celebration of the marriage between form and function, a guide to crafting messages that not only capture attention, but captivate the soul.

Here, you'll learn from the masters of the craft, who remind us that true creativity isn't just about being different - it's about being relentlessly *effective*.

Words That Move Mountains

Our odyssey concludes with the art of **COPY**. The power of words.

Here, we delve into the essence of communication, exploring how the right words, when put together with knowledge, purpose and passion, can indeed move mountains.

This section is a homage to the power of persuasive language and its ability to generate monumental results.

It is a testament to the fact that words, when wielded with skill and empathy, can touch hearts, change minds and inspire actions.

As you turn these pages, let each quotation be a stepping stone, a spark and a realisation.

Whether you're seeking guidance, inspiration, or simply a moment of reflection, this book will be a constant companion for your journey towards excellence.

So, embark on this adventure with an open heart and a curious mind.

Be ready to be inspired - to change - and to soar.

Here's to the power of words, the beauty of creativity and the unending quest for greatness.

Welcome to your odyssey...

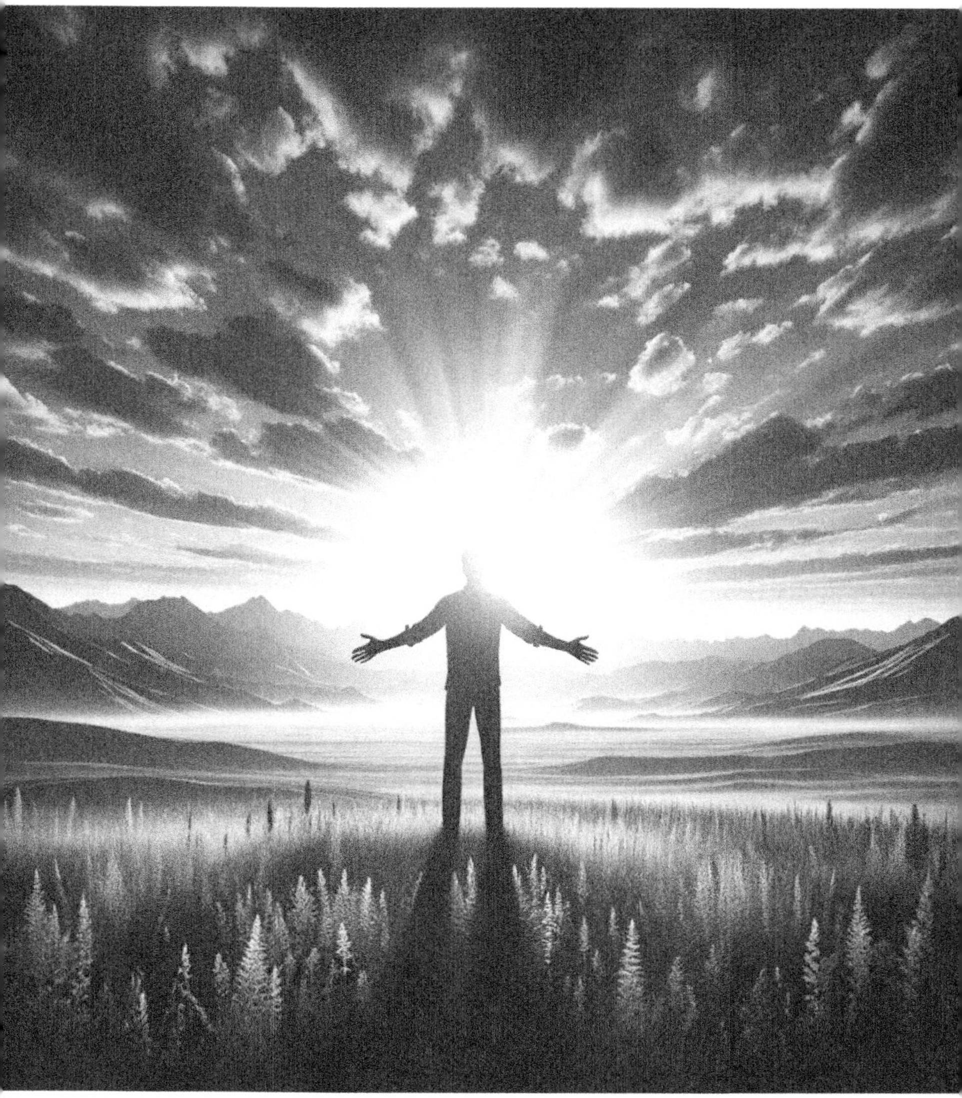

SECTION 1 – ADVICE & INSPIRATION

It doesn't get any better than this. It can't. It's impossible.

You are, effectively, opening a door and walking into a room that contains the most talented, legendary individuals that have ever walked the earth.

They are giants. *Titans*. Every one of them.

And they are waiting to greet you and shower you with advice, inspiration and direction - that will not only make you think, it will help you grow, develop and be better at what you do.

There are 10 sections within this first category. They are:

Persistence and Resilience

Customer Focus and Marketing

Creativity and Originality

Leadership, Success and Failure

Personal Development and Growth

Business and Strategy

Life, Philosophy, Wisdom and Knowledge

Humour and Perspective

Critical Views and Commentary

Inspirational and Motivational

In these sections, you will hear wisdom of the very highest order, freely given by leaders, thinkers and visionaries, whose voices have been loud and clear throughout the challenges of time.

Let them light your path to personal excellence and inspire you to realise your potential.

Persistence and Resilience

'I've always been greatly moved by people with incredible mental strength.

Individuals that continue to push, no matter how hard they fall. This section is a tribute to people with that indomitable spirit. Surviving is a noble fight, as someone much smarter than me, once said. But to some people, surviving isn't enough. To these extraordinary people, life is all about turning challenges into opportunities - and thriving as a result.

The voices you'll find here, have walked through fire and emerged stronger. They remind us that every setback is a setup for a comeback.'

> "A river cuts through rock, not because of its power, but because of its persistence." **Jim Watkins**
>
> "A winner is just a loser who tried one more time." **George M. Moore Jr.**
>
> "Big shots are only little shots who keep shooting." **Christopher Morley**
>
> "Doing advertising is like Joe Louis. Jab, jab, jab. Find an opening, then pow. Then pour it on. That's how it ought to go, I think. One ad ain't a panacea. You've got to jab a lot and wait for your moment." **George Tannenbaum**
>
> "Don't listen to anyone who tells you that you can't do this or that. That's nonsense. Make up your mind, you'll never use crutches or a stick, then have a go at everything. Go to school, join in all the games you can. Go anywhere you want to. But never, never let them persuade you that things are too difficult or impossible." **Douglas Bader**
>
> "Everyone wants to climb the mountain, but the big difference between those at the top and those still on the bottom, is simply a matter of showing up tomorrow to give it just one more shot." **Gary Halbert**

"Don't watch the clock; do what it does. Keep going." **Sam Levenson**

"Do you think I look like this naturally? I work. I work eight hours a day to look like this." **Cindy Crawford**

"Endurance is not just the ability to bear a hard thing, but to turn it into glory." **William Barclay**

"Energy and persistence conquer all things." **Benjamin Franklin**

"Failure is not the opposite of success; it's part of success." **Arianna Huffington**

"Genius is 1% inspiration and 99% perspiration." **Thomas Edison**

"Great works are performed not by strength, but by perseverance." **Samuel Johnson**

"I am hitting my head against the walls, but the walls are giving way." **Gustav Mahler**

"I have no secret. There are no rules to follow in business. I just work hard and, as I always have done, believe I can do it. Most of all, though, I try to have fun." **Richard Branson**

"I've missed more than 9,000 shots in my career. I've lost almost 300 games. 26 times, I've been trusted to take the game-winning shot and missed. I've failed over and over and over again in my life. And that is why I succeed." **Michael Jordan**

"If you're going through hell, keep going." **Winston Churchill**

"It always seems impossible until it's done." **Nelson Mandela**

"My greatest point is my persistence. I never give up in a match. However down I am, I fight until the last ball. My list of matches shows that I have turned a great many so-called irretrievable defeats into victories." **Bjorn Borg**

"Never, never, *never* give up." **Winston Churchill**

"Obstacles don't have to stop you. If you run into a wall, don't turn around and give up. Figure out how to climb it, go through it, or work around it." **Michael Jordan**

"Once you start believing in yourself, anything is possible. Once you start believing in yourself, your dreams take shape. The more you believe, the more you achieve." **Martina Navratilova**

"Only those who dare to fail greatly can ever achieve greatly." **Robert F. Kennedy**

"Perseverance, the secret of all triumphs." **Victor Hugo**

"Persist, push, hang on, keep going, never give up. When the man says no, pretend you can't hear him. Look confused, stammer, say "Huh?" Persistence - it's a cliché, but it happens to work. The person who makes it, is the person who keeps going after everyone else has quit. This is more important than intelligence, pedigree, even connections. Be dogged. Keep hitting that door until you bust it down." **Jerry Weintraub**

"Press on. Nothing in the world can take the place of persistence. Talent will not; nothing is more common than unsuccessful men with talent. Genius will not; unrewarded genius is almost a proverb. Education alone will not, the world is full of educated derelicts. Persistence and determination alone are omnipotent." **Calvin Coolidge**

"If you don't push timidity into a corner, it will push you into a corner." **Jim Rohn**

"Put your head down and work hard. Never wait for things to happen, make them happen for yourself, through hard graft and not giving up." **Gordon Ramsay**

"Rock bottom became the solid foundation on which I rebuilt my life." **J.K. Rowling**

"Success is not achieved by winning all the time. Real success comes when we rise after we fall. Some mountains are higher than others. Some roads steeper than the next. There are hardships and setbacks but you cannot let them stop you. Even on the steepest road you must not turn back." **Muhammad Ali**

"Success is not the absence of failure; it's the persistence through failure." **Aisha Tyler**

"Take the first step, and your mind will mobilize all its forces to your aid. But the first essential is that you begin. Once the battle is started, all that is within and without you will come to your assistance." **Robert Collier**

"The future belongs to those who believe in the beauty of their dreams." **Eleanor Roosevelt**

"The greatest glory in living lies not in never falling, but in rising every time we fall." **Nelson Mandela**

"The master has failed more times than the beginner has even tried." **Stephen McCranie**

"The only way to achieve the impossible, is to believe it is possible." **Charles Kingsleigh**

"There is no job so small that you can afford to overlook it, or any challenge so large that you should be afraid to face it." **Stanley Marcus**

"There is nothing impossible to him who will try." **Alexander the Great**

"Through perseverance, many people win success out of what seemed destined to be certain failure." **Benjamin Disraeli**

"What does not kill me, makes me stronger." **Friedrich Nietzsche**

"When you come to the end of your rope, tie a knot and hang on." **Franklin D. Roosevelt**

"You can get it if you really want, but you must try, try and try, try and try, you'll succeed at last." **Jimmy Cliff**

"When everything seems to be going against you, remember that the airplane takes off against the wind, not with it." **Henry Ford**

Customer Focus and Marketing

This is where the heart meets the hustle.

Understanding and serving our customers is the foundation of any successful endeavour. There is absolutely no doubt about that at all. Yet, more people than ever these days, care little about customers - and this is proven, by them spending, on average, 7 times more on getting new customers, than on the ones they already have.

Big mistake.

These showcased insights cut to the core of genuine customer connection - because marketing, at its best, isn't about transactions. It's about understanding customers, by listening to them and giving them what they want - not what we *think* they want.'

"All business success rests on something labelled a sale, which at least momentarily, weds company and customer." **Tom Peters**

"Always remember this key fact. It's not the quality of the service that you give, but the quality of the service the customer perceives, that makes that customer happy. Customers are like hearts. They go where they're appreciated." **Andy Owen**

"Always talk up to your prospects, not down. When flattered, people almost always rise to the occasion." **Ray Jutkins**

"Consumers don't want a social purpose, but they want cheaper." **Steve Harrison**

"Customer satisfaction is worthless. Customer loyalty is priceless." **Jeffrey Gitomer**

"I realise that the next sale begins, the minute I deliver the new car." **Joe Girard**

"In the sales profession, the real work begins after the sale is made." **Brian Tracy**

"Customers have different names, ages, addresses, dialects, education, incomes, ethnic backgrounds, experiences, aspirations, circumstances, family structure, motivations, behaviour patterns, personalities, character traits, physical features, emotional makeups and personal priorities. Consumers are individuals as unique as snowflakes." **Jerry Reitman**

"If you make a customer happy, they will tell three other people how good you are. If you make the customer unhappy, they will tell eleven people how bad you are." **Murray Raphel**

"If you want to be more successful, try marketing to the *differences* of people, not their *similarities*. But you'll need to discover what those differences are, before you start writing a single word." **Andy Owen**

"In marketing, I've seen only one strategy that can't miss - and that is to market to your best customers first, your best prospects second and the rest of the world last." **John Romero**

"In tough times, it's your existing customers that will keep you warm." **Andy Owen**

"Keep on telling your story. As often as you can. Remind your customers who you are and what you offer. This is absolutely necessary, because if you forget to remind your customers who you are and what you offer, they will simply stop coming back." **Murray Raphel**

"Let your clients and customers know you care. Reach out and touch them. Hold their hand. Be their teddy bear. Be their security blanket. Demonstrate *love*." **Ray Jutkins**

"Loyalty is not won by being first. It is won by being best." **Stefan Persson**

"Make your pitch as emotional as possible. Cartesian logic sells few widgets." **Denny Hatch**

"Legendary direct marketer Bob Hemmings once worked for a jeweller on New York's West 47th Street diamond district, where the merchant's rent counters and window space in a kind of a giant co-op. Every evening all the jewellers would dutifully take their diamonds out of the showcases and lock them in the safe until the next morning. All the jewellers, that is, except for Hemming's boss, who would leave his diamonds out all night and put his customer list in the safe. *'If I lose the diamonds, the insurance company will pay,'* he told Hemmings. *'If I lose my customer list, I am out of business'.*" **Denny Hatch**

"Make a clear offer – the strongest one possible - and do not give your reader many choices. 'You cannot sell two things at once,' as Dick Benson never tired of observing." **Denny Hatch**

"Our first duty is not to the old sales curve - it is to the audience." **Howard Gossage**

"People don't go on *'customer journeys.'* This is a marketing buzzword designed to make the user sound sophisticated – it's complete bollocks. There are only two contact strategies to use, and they're linked to the most relevant touch-points. After all, a prospect isn't a customer until they buy something: *Prospect contact strategy* - to generate new customers. *Customer contact strategy* – to keep profitable customers and generate referrals." **Malcolm Auld**

"Why do customers leave you? Several independent surveys asking this same question were done - and amazingly, all came with nearly identical responses. 14% left because of complaints not taken care of. 9% left for the competition. 9% moved out of town. 68% said they left for "no special reason." In other words, seven out of ten people who were "steady" customers said they left for "no special reason." I don't believe that. I think there was a reason. I think the reason was, the business did not keep in touch with them. They took them for granted. And when someone is taken for granted - they don't feel important and are susceptible to the next mating cry." **Murray Raphel**

"People don't care how much you know until they know how much you care." **Theodore Roosevelt**

"Remember, people do not buy red buttons. They buy what happens when you push red buttons." **Ray Jutkins**

"If there is no offer, there will be no sale." **Andy Owen**

"Spend your money where it does the most good - your customers." **Drayton Bird**

"The best advertising is done by satisfied customers." **Philip Kotler**

"The aim of marketing is to know and understand the customer so well, the product or service fits him and sells itself." **Peter Drucker**

"The best marketing doesn't feel like marketing." **Tom Fishburne**

"The best way to find yourself is to lose yourself in the service of others." **Mahatma Gandhi**

"The customer or prospect doesn't give a damn about you, your company, or your product. All that matters is *'What's in it for me?'* **Bob Hacker**

"The key to getting your email opened can be described in one word – 'trust' Without trust, your recipient won't open your email. They'll trust you if they know who you are and understand why you are contacting them. But if what you type in the two fields of the heading 'From' and 'Subject' don't engender trust – you'll get deleted as quick as blinking." **Malcolm Auld**

"The object of this business is not to make money. The object of this business is to serve its customers. The *result* is to make money." **John Frazer Robinson**

"The purpose of business is to create and keep a customer." **Professor Theodore Levitt**

"The objective of all advertising is to buy new customers at a profit. Learn what your customers cost and what they buy - spend all of your ammunition where it counts." **Claude Hopkins**

"The purpose of business, is to sell more stuff to more people, more often, for more money." **Sergio Zyman**

"Don't find customers for your products, find products for your customers." **Seth Godin**

"The rewarded customer buys, multiplies and comes back." **Dr Michael Lebeouf**

"The sale merely consummates the courtship, at which point the marriage begins." **Professor Theodore Levitt**

"The simple formula for business success. Have more customers. Have your customers shop more often. Have them buy more when they come in." **John Groman**

"The single most important skill you need to be successful in selling, is the ability to listen to your customer. There's an old Irish proverb that says it well: *'Listen to the sound of the river and you will catch fish.'* That means you must always 'listen' to your customer. Do that well and they will continue to buy from you, because they will know you are answering their needs." **Feargal Quinn**

"The strongest brand is the brand with the most customers. They pay more and they stay longer." **Professor Andrew Ehrenberg**

"The three goals of your marketing communications - and there are only three - acquire new customers, get customers to spend more money with you more often - and get customers to keep spending with you for as long as possible. If your marketing communications are not helping you achieve one or more of these goals, you're probably wasting your money, regardless of the media channels or vanity metrics you use." **Malcolm Auld**

"We are so busy talking, that we don't find the time to listen. And if we do not listen, we cannot find out what our customers want." **Murray Raphel**

"There is only one profit centre in business. It is your customer." **Peter Drucker**

"We see our customers as invited guests to a party - and we are the hosts. It's our job to make the customer experience a little bit better." **Jeff Bezos**

"Whatever your product, however impressive your expertise, people will never care how much you know until they know how much you care." **Gary Bencivenga**

"When you give people rational, logical and honest-to-goodness reasons to act in their own self-interest -*voila* -they do! What's more, it's the best kind of sale you can make, because it's a sale built on mutual benefit, trust and the truth, all of which will endow you with future sales from that same customer." **Gary Bencivenga**

"You've got to start with the customer experience and work back toward the technology, not the other way around." **Steve Jobs**

"Your competitors won't put you out of business. But your customers certainly will. So, stop worrying about your competitors and concentrate more on your customers." **Andy Owen**

"Your customers want to buy when they want to buy, not when you want to sell." **Murray Raphel**

"The customer you've got, is 4 - 5 times more likely to buy from you than someone identical who is not a customer. A previous enquirer is about twice as likely to buy. A past customer is usually your next best bet." **Drayton Bird**

Creativity and Originality

We have to all suffer so much crap. It's everywhere you look these days.

It is a morass of mediocrity.

To rise above the general noise level, is vitally important. You need to unleash your own creative spirit and leave your unique mark on the world.

In this section, I celebrate the mavericks and the dreamers. People who dare to think differently.

These are wise words from individuals whose vision didn't just push boundaries - they shattered them.'

> "A good artist should be isolated. If he isn't isolated, something is wrong." **Orson Welles**

> "A good composer does not imitate; he steals." **Igor Stravinsky**

> "A USP has three parts: Each ad must make a proposition – 'Buy this product and you get these benefits.' The proposition must be unique - something that your competitors do not, cannot or will not offer. The proposition must sell - it must be something prospects really want; it pulls them over to your product. In essence, a USP briefly and clearly explains a single quality about your product that lets it stand out against the competition." **Rosser Reeves**

> "All good ideas start out as bad ideas, that's why it takes so long." **Steven Spielberg**

> "Bad artists copy. Good artists steal." **Pablo Picasso**

> "Big is rarely beautiful – or smart. Showing imagination, using knowledge and common sense and being flexible, are more often to be found in the small and nimble. And long may it continue." **Drayton Bird**

"Chance favours the prepared mind." **Louis Pasteur**

"Conformity is the last refuge of the unimaginative." **Oscar Wilde**

"Creativity is allowing yourself to make mistakes. Art is knowing which ones to keep." **Scott Adams**

"Creativity is the power to reject the past, to change the status quo - and to seek new potential." **Ai Weiwei**

"Excellence isn't an act, it's a habit." **Quincy Jones**

"Figure out what you do that other people don't, can't or won't do. Then make that something your unique selling proposition." **George Tannenbaum**

"Great spirits have always found violent opposition from mediocrities." **Albert Einstein**

"If it's been done, do it better. If it hasn't been done, do it so well, that better is not an option." **Lee Clow**

"If someone tells you they will "build you a brand" they're talking nonsense. Only *you* can build your brand. Be special - offer something no one else does. Do things your competitors don't. Do them in a way they don't." **Drayton Bird**

"Imagination is everything. It is the preview of life's coming attractions." **Albert Einstein**

"Innovation distinguishes between a leader and a follower." **Steve Jobs**

"Originality is nothing but judicious imitation." **Voltaire**

"Originality is the fine art of remembering what you hear but forgetting where you heard it." **Laurence J. Peter**

"People who say it cannot be done, should not interrupt those who are doing it." **George Bernard Shaw**

"Simplicity is the ultimate sophistication." **Leonardo Da Vinci**

"Talent borrows. Genius steals." **Oscar Wilde**

"The chief enemy of creativity is 'good' sense." **Pablo Picasso**

"The Duke of Wellington was asked to what he owed his victories. *'Attention to detail,'* he replied." **Drayton Bird**

"The principal mark of genius is not perfection, but originality, the opening of new frontiers." **Arthur Koestler**

"The worst enemy to creativity is self-doubt." **Sylvia Plath**

"There are only 2 basic ways to establish competitive advantage: do things better than others, or do them differently." **Karl Albrecht**

"There is a master key to success which no man can fail. Its name is simplicity." **Henry Detterding**

"Times change. People don't." **John Caples**

"To live a creative life, we must lose our fear of being wrong." **Joseph Chilton Pearce**

"What makes a good client? Willingness to test." **Drayton Bird**

"When you position yourself, your company, your product and your offer, as a leader - and can prove it, not just say it - you will be way ahead of the game. And your competition." **Ray Jutkins**

"Without deviation from the norm, progress is not possible." **Frank Zappa**

"You can't use up creativity. The more you use, the more you have." **Maya Angelou**

"You won't get anything, unless you have the vision to imagine it." **John Lennon**

"Without freedom, there is no creation." **Jiddu Krishnamurti**

"While direct mail usually costs more to create, it almost always has far higher response rates than any online advertising. A piece of mail is a complete advertisement. Mail has the highest attention rate of any media. Yet, most marketers haven't realised that when it comes to direct or unaddressed mail, that the media is the message." **Malcolm Auld**

"The man who follows the crowd will usually get no further than the crowd. The man who walks alone, is likely to find himself in places no one has ever been." **Albert Einstein**

"Don't wait for inspiration. It comes while working." **Henri Matisse**

"Nothing is original. Steal from anywhere that resonates with inspiration or fuels your imagination. Devour old films, new films, music, books, paintings, photographs, poems, dreams, random conversations, architecture, bridges, street signs, trees, clouds, bodies of water, light and shadows. Select only things to steal from that speak directly to your soul. If you do this, your work (and theft) will be authentic. Authenticity is invaluable; originality is non-existent. And don't bother concealing your thievery - celebrate it if you feel like it." **Jim Jarmusch**

"It's not where you take things from - it's where you take them." **Jean-Luc Godard**

Leadership, Success & Failure

'Some lead. Most follow.

Leaders are giants. Titans. They inspire. They motivate. And they succeed.

And that inspiration moves others to do extraordinary things and be successful, too. But success often comes hand-in-hand with lessons learned from failure.

In this section, you'll find wisdom from those who've navigated the stormy seas of leadership, showing us that true success is forged through resilience, learning from our mistakes - and leading with courage and integrity.'

> "It is the responsibility of leadership to work intelligently with what is given, and not waste time fantasizing about a world of flawless people and perfect choices." **Marcus Aurelius**

> "A genuine leader is not a searcher for consensus, but a moulder of consensus." **Martin Luther King Jr.**

> "A leader is a dealer in hope." **Napoleon**

> "Do not be embarrassed by your failures, learn from them and start again." **Richard Branson**

> "Do not judge me by my successes, judge me by how many times I fell down and got back up again." **Nelson Mandela**

> "Do what you do best, and outsource the rest." **Peter Drucker**

> "Failing often, and testing big differences, shows you are trying hard enough." **Gene Schwartz**

> "Failure is a detour, not a dead-end street." **Zig Ziglar**

> "Failure is simply the opportunity to begin again, this time more intelligently." **Henry Ford**

> "I can accept failure; everyone fails at something. But I can't accept not trying." **Michael Jordan**

"I learned that good judgment comes from experience and that experience grows out of mistakes." **Omar N. Bradley**

"I would rather be first in a small village in Gaul than second in command in Rome." **Julius Caesar**

"If you ever find a man who is better than you are - hire him. If necessary, pay him more than you pay yourself." **David Ogilvy**

"If you want others to like you, if you want to develop real friendships, if you want to help others at the same time as you help yourself, keep this principle in mind: Become genuinely interested in other people." **Dale Carnegie**

"If you want to increase your success rate, double your failure rate." **Thomas J. Watson**

"In the real world, the smartest people are people who make mistakes and learn. In school, the smartest people don't make mistakes." **Robert T. Kiyosaki**

"It's fine to celebrate success, but it is more important to heed the lessons of failure." **Bill Gates**

"Leadership and learning are indispensable to each other." **John F. Kennedy**

"Leadership is not about being in charge. It is about taking care of those in your charge." **Simon Sinek**

"Leadership is the art of getting someone else to do something you want done because he wants to do it." **Dwight D. Eisenhower**

"Leadership is the capacity to translate vision into reality." **Warren Bennis**

"My job is not to be easy on people. My job is to make them better." **Steve Jobs**

"My mistakes are my life." **Samuel Beckett**

"My biggest successes and advances in direct marketing, have universally come from defeat. Because I was that much tougher to beat the next time. You can emulate this every time you experience a setback in your own marketing. Mark my words, your setbacks will yield the secrets of your greatest breakthroughs." **Gary Bencivenga**

"Success has many fathers, but failure is an orphan." **John F. Kennedy**

"Success is not final; failure is not fatal: It is the courage to continue that counts." **Winston Churchill**

"Success is not how high you have climbed, but how you make a positive difference to the world." **Roy T. Bennett**

"Success is the ability to go from one failure to another with no loss of enthusiasm." **Winston Churchill**

"Success usually comes to those who are too busy to be looking for it." **Henry David Thoreau**

"The competitor to be feared, is one who never bothers about you at all, but goes on making his own business better all the time." **Henry Ford**

"The function of leadership is to produce more leaders, not more followers." **Ralph Nader**

"The leader of the past was a person who knew how to tell. The leader of the future will be a person who knows how to ask." **Peter Drucker**

"The only place where success comes before work, is in the dictionary." **Vidal Sassoon**

"The policy of being too cautious is the greatest risk of all." **Jawaharlal Nehru**

"There is nothing on earth that you cannot have, once you have mentally accepted the fact that you can have it." **Robert Collier**

"To handle yourself, use your head; to handle others, use your heart." **Eleanor Roosevelt**

"Twenty years from now, you will be more disappointed by the things that you didn't do than by the ones you did do." **Mark Twain**

"We learn as professionals by repetition, by getting it wrong, getting yelled at - and doing it again." **Anthony Bourdain**

"When all think alike, then no one is thinking." **Walter Lippman**

"When you lose, don't lose the lesson." **Dalai Lama**

"Whether you think you can or you think you can't, you're right." **Henry Ford**

"You build on failure. You use it as a stepping stone. Close the door on the past. You don't try to forget the mistakes, but you don't dwell on it. You don't let it have any of your energy, or any of your time, or any of your space." **Johnny Cash**

"You don't learn to walk by following rules. You learn by doing, and by falling over." **Richard Branson**

"You have to find it. No one else can find it for you." **Bjorn Borg**

"You have to take your knocks before you can appreciate what success is all about." **Eddy Boas**

"If you don't risk anything, you risk even more." **Erica Jong**

"The most difficult thing is the decision to act, the rest is merely tenacity." **Amelia Earhart**

"When we strive to become better than we are, everything around us becomes better too." **Paulo Coelho**

"One life is all we have and we live it as we believe in living it. But to sacrifice what you are and to live without belief, that is a fate more terrible than dying." **Joan of Arc**

Personal Development and Growth

'On our journey to becoming better in everything we do, every single step counts.

This collection of wise words, is close to my heart, offering the very finest guidance and wisdom for personal growth.

It's about self-reflection, embracing change and the continuous journey of learning, evolving and improving.

If these legendary voices don't inspire you to grow, challenge yourself and chase after the best version of who you can be, then there is no hope for you.'

"A life spent making mistakes is not only more honourable, but more useful than a life spent doing nothing." **George Bernard Shaw**

"A man can succeed at almost anything for which he has unlimited enthusiasm." **Charles Schwab**

"A man is a success if he gets up in the morning and gets to bed at night - and in between he does what he wants to do." **Bob Dylan**

"A man only learns in two ways, one by reading, and the other by association with smarter people." **Will Rogers**

"Become a student of change. It is the only thing that will remain constant." **Anthony D'Angelo**

"Change is the end result of all true learning." **Leo Buscaglia**

"Do not go where the path may lead, go instead where there is no path and leave a trail." **Ralph Waldo Emerson**

"Do not let what you cannot do, interfere with what you can do." **John Wooden**

"Don't go through life, grow through life." **Eric Butterworth**

"Do what you feel in your heart to be right - for you'll be criticized anyway." **Eleanor Roosevelt**

"Don't let negative and toxic people rent space in your head. Raise the rent and kick them out." **Zig Ziglar**

"Educating the mind without educating the heart is no education at all." **Aristotle**

"Every minute doing one thing, is a minute not doing something else. Every choice is another choice not made, another path grown over, lost." **Jerry Weintraub**

"Five years from now, you're the same person except for the people you've met and the books you've read." **John Wooden**

"Growth and comfort do not coexist." **Ginni Rometty**

"He began to acquire knowledge. Which is how an ordinary man becomes a titan. If you want to learn, find a person who knows - and study him or her." **Jerry Weintraub**

"He who has a *why* to live can bear almost any *how*." **Friedrich Nietzsche**

"He who is not busy being born, is busy dying." **Bob Dylan**

"I am a part of everything that I have read." **Roosevelt**

"I do not think much of a man who is not wiser today than he was yesterday." **Abraham Lincoln**

"I keep six honest serving-men (they taught me all I knew). Their names are What and Why and When and How and Where and Who." **Rudyard Kipling**

"I may not have gone where I intended to go, but I think I have ended up where I needed to be." **Douglas Adams**

"If we encounter a man of rare intellect, we should ask him what books he reads." **Ralph Waldo Emerson**

"If you don't work passionately and furiously at being the best in the world at what you do - then you fail your talent, your destiny and your God." **George Lois**

"If you want to be the best, baby, you've got to work harder than anybody else." **Sammy Davis Jr.**

"If you want to fly, give up everything that weighs you down." **Buddha**

"If you want to improve how you manage time - stop doing what doesn't need to be done!" **Peter Drucker**

"It seems that the more places I see and experience, the bigger I realize the world to be. The more I become aware of, the more I realize how relatively little I know of it, how many places I have still to go, how much more there is to learn. Maybe that's enlightenment enough - to know that there is no final resting place of the mind, no moment of smug clarity. Perhaps wisdom, at least for me, means realizing how small and unwise I am - and how far I have yet to go." **Anthony Bourdain**

"It's only after you've stepped outside your comfort zone, that you begin to change, grow, and transform." **Roy T. Bennett**

"It's what you learn after you know it all that counts." **John Wooden**

"It's no good being too easily swayed by people's opinions. You have to believe in yourself." **Donatella Versace**

"Keep the circus going inside you, keep it going, don't take anything too seriously, it'll all work out in the end." **David Niven**

"Knowing yourself is the beginning of all wisdom." **Aristotle**

"Learning from case studies and theories and concepts and the long and rich history of marketing - which stretches out across a wonderful century of application - is worthy of all of us. I think that anyone that actually tries to argue that studying marketing is a waste of time is, well, a Philistine." **Mark Ritson**

"Listening is a basic survival skill. If you can't listen, you can't learn. A study at the University of Minnesota showed that 60% of business misunderstanding is due to poor listening." **Ray Jutkins**

"Live as if you were to die tomorrow. Learn as if you were to live forever." **Mahatma Gandhi**

"Most people work at keeping their job, rather than doing a good job. If you're the former, you're leading a meaningless life. If you're the latter, keep up the good work." **George Lois**

"No matter what the situation, remind yourself: I have a choice." **Deepak Chopra**

"One of the best ways to persuade others is with your ears - by listening to them." **Dean Rusk**

"People will tell you where they've gone, they'll tell you where to go - but until you get there for yourself, you never really know." **Joni Mitchell**

"Personal development is your springboard to personal excellence. Ongoing, continuous, non-stop personal development literally assures you that there is no limit to what you can accomplish." **Brian Tracy**

"Playing safe is probably the most unsafe thing in the world. You cannot stand still. You must go forward." **Robert Collier**

"Regret is something you've got to just live with, you can't drink it away. You can't run away from it. You can't trick yourself out of it. You've just got to own it." **Anthony Bourdain**

"Skills are cheap. Passion is priceless." **Gary Vaynerchuk**

"Stop taking yourself so seriously. You really aren't that important. Your passing may leave a vacuum, but it will be filled quicker than you would ever believe. I don't say this to put you down. The real message here is - *Get out there and start having some fun!*" **Gary Halbert**

"The only person you are destined to become, is the person you decide to be." **Ralph Waldo Emerson**

"The only thing standing between you and your goal is the story you keep telling yourself as to why you can't achieve it." **Jordan Belfort**

"The wise man does not grow old, but ripens." **Victor Hugo**

"There is nothing noble in being superior to your fellow man; true nobility is being superior to your former self." **Ernest Hemingway**

"Thinking: the talking of the soul with itself." **Plato**

"To achieve great things, two things are needed; a plan, and not quite enough time." **Leonard Bernstein**

"Whatever you are, be a good one." **Abraham Lincoln**

"When things are tough, I have discovered that a very, very simple (but effective) thing to do, is just keep moving in some sort of positive direction." **Gary Halbert**

"When you're good at something, make that *everything*." **Roger Federer**

"You are never too old to set another goal or to dream a new dream." **C.S. Lewis**

"You are no better than anyone else and no one is better than you." **John Wooden**

"You can make more friends in two months by being interested in other people, than you can in two years by trying to get other people interested in you." **Dale Carnegie**

"Surround yourself with people who have similar goals or who have already become great successes." **Gary Halbert**

"You don't stumble upon your heritage. It's there, just waiting to be explored and shared." **Robbie Robertson**

"Well, you know, a lot of people look at the negative things, the things that they did wrong and, I do, too. But I like to stress on the things I did right, because there are certain things that I like to look at from a positive standpoint that are just positive reinforcement." **Tiger Woods**

"You must always strive to be the best, but you must never believe that you are." **Juan Manuel Fangio**

"The one thing that you have that nobody else has is you. Your voice, your mind, your story, your vision. So, write and draw and build and play and dance and live, only as you can." **Neil Gaiman**

Business and Strategy

'Being a success in business and life is bloody hard.

In fact, it's probably never been harder than it is now. So much noise, so much information and so much choice, make it more difficult than ever to stand out and make a difference.

You need talent, vision and adaptability. To see beyond the horizon and crafting plans that can turn that vision into reality. Like the people below, who share their insights with us.

They are winners who've mastered the challenges in front of them, using strategic wisdom that transcends the ordinary.'

> "A good plan violently executed today, is far and away better than a perfect plan tomorrow." **George S. Patton**
>
> "All business is global business." **Kenichi Ohmae**
>
> "Business has only two functions - marketing and innovation." **Milan Kundera**
>
> "Business is like war in one respect. If its grand strategy is correct, any number of tactical errors can be made and yet the enterprise proves successful." **General Robert E. Woods**
>
> "Business opportunities are like buses, there's always another one coming." **Richard Branson**
>
> "Confidence comes from being prepared." **John Wooden**
>
> "Don't delay acting on a good idea. Chances are someone else has just thought of it, too. Success comes to the one who acts first." **H. Jackson Brown, Jr.**
>
> "Every problem is a gift - without problems we would not grow." **Anthony Robbins**
>
> "Great things are done by a series of small things brought together." **Vincent Van Gogh**

"I find that the harder I work, the more luck I seem to have." **Thomas Jefferson**

"If you are serious about your business, then be serious about your approach. Don't accept second best. Especially when it comes to the art of selling. Employ people who know how it's done." **Andy Owen**

"If you do one significant thing better each year, you have a fair chance of outdoing your competitors. If you do two, you almost certainly will. If you do three, you'll wipe the floor with them." **Drayton Bird**

"If your service is too generous, your clients will love you, but you will go broke." **David Ogilvy**

"In the world of business, the people who are most successful are those who are doing what they love." **Warren Buffet**

"It's not very clever when you pay too much, but it's brainless when you pay too little. When you pay too much, you lose a little money, but, when you pay too little, you will almost certainly lose loads." **Andy Owen**

"It's the little details that are vital. Little things make big things happen." **John Wooden**

"Loyalty is what is left when the bribes are taken away." **Victor Ross**

"Marketing is no longer about the stuff that you make, but about the stories you tell." **Seth Godin**

"Never do anything yourself that you can hire someone else to do, especially if they can do it better." **Bill Bernbach**

"Not spending enough money on your marketing programme, is just like buying an airline ticket half way to the Far East. You will spend a lot, but you don't get where you want to go." **Ray Jutkins**

"Margins have absolutely nothing to do with success. What is important, is perceived value and the effectiveness of your advertising message. It is the need you have created, the exclusivity of the product you are offering - and the ease in which people can obtain it." **Murray Raphel**

"Marketing is really just about sharing your passion." **Michael Hyatt**

"Nothing happens in business until something gets sold." **Thomas Watson Jr - Chairman of IBM**

"Outstanding people have one thing in common: An absolute sense of mission." **Zig Ziglar**

"Preparation, I have often said, is rightly two-thirds of any venture." **Amelia Earhart**

"Risk more than others think is safe. Dream more than others think is practical." **Howard Schultz**

"Since the ad industry isn't responsible enough to stop tracking, it must be outlawed." **Bob Hoffman**

"Strategy is all very well, but it pays to give thought from time to time, to the results." **Winston Churchill**

"Strategy is choosing what not to do." **Michael Porter**

"Strategy without tactics is the slowest route to victory. Tactics without strategy is the noise before defeat." **Sun Tzu**

"The aim of marketing is to make selling superfluous." **Peter Drucker**

"The best investment you can make is in yourself." **Warren Buffett**

"The common law of business balance prohibits paying a little and getting a lot - it can't be done." **John Ruskin**

"The eight laws of learning are explanation, demonstration, imitation, repetition, repetition, repetition, repetition, repetition." **John Wooden**

"The essence of strategy is choosing what not to do." **Michael Porter**

"The only way to influence someone, is to find out what they want, and show them how to get it." **Dale Carnegie**

"There are four decisions for business success. 1. Decide what you want to do. 2. Decide what you'll give up to get it. 3. Decide your priorities. 4. Decide to do it!" **H.L. Hunt, Texas Oil Billionaire**

"There are no secrets to success. It is the result of preparation, hard work - and learning from failure." **Colin Powell**

"There's no mystery to this business. It's just logic." **Herschell Gordon Lewis**

"Your brand is what other people say about you when you're not in the room." **Jeff Bezos**

"Your first aim in business is to avoid making a loss." **Peter Drucker**

"A businessman is no different from any other kind." **Robert Collier**

Life, Philosophy, Wisdom & Knowledge

'Life's big questions and the search for meaning, have always fascinated me.

I'm sure they have fascinated you, too.

This section dives deep into the essence of being, offering philosophical insights and wisdom that spans centuries.

It's a reminder to pause, reflect and greatly appreciate the depth and richness of the human experience.'

"A mistake is only an error. It becomes a mistake when you fail to correct it." **John Lennon**

"A neat stall is the sign of a dead horse." **David Ogilvy**

"A passion for pleasure is the secret of remaining young." **Oscar Wilde**

"A pessimist sees the difficulty in every opportunity; an optimist sees the opportunity in every difficulty." **Winston Churchill**

"Better to fight for something, than live for nothing." **George S. Patton**

"Do the steps that you've been shown, by everyone you've ever known, until the dance becomes your very own." **Jackson Browne**

"Don't hide your scars. They make you who you are." **Frank Sinatra**

"Don't bend; don't water it down; don't try to make it logical; don't edit your own soul according to the fashion. Rather, follow your most intense obsessions mercilessly." **Franz Kafka**

"Don't it always seem to go, that you don't know what you've got till it's gone." **Joni Mitchell**

"Everything you do is insignificant. Yet, it's vitally important that you do it." **Gandhi**

"Follow your bliss. That which you love you must spend your life doing, as passionately and as perfectly as your heart, mind and instincts allow. The sooner you identify that bliss, which surely resides in the soul of most human beings, the greater your chance of a truly successful life. In the act of creativity, being careful guarantees sameness and mediocrity, which means your work will be invisible. Better to be reckless than careful. Better to be bold than safe. Better to have your work seen and remembered, or you've struck out. There is no middle ground." **George Lois**

"Follow your heart, listen to your inner voice, stop caring about what others think." **Roy T. Bennett**

"Develop the habit of divine discontent. Set your sights high, blaze new trails, compete with the immortals." **David Ogilvy**

"Fear kills more people than death." **George S. Patton**

"Follow your heart. Your brain is the smartest organ in your body, but your heart is the wisest. In any activity, whether in marketing or in life, listen to your heart. If your heart is saying one thing, but your brain (or the "expert" running the meeting) is forcing the issue in another direction, take a step back and listen to that voice from your heart. Don't be afraid of that inner voice. It is not just your best friend. It is *you*. You will live a much happier life, be much more influential and become a much better marketer because other people's hearts vibrate to the same string. The more you listen to your own heart, the more you will hear and influence the hearts of others." **Gary Bencivenga**

"He who knows others is wise; he who knows himself is enlightened." **Lao Tzu**

"I let negativity roll off me like water off a duck's back. If it's not positive, I don't hear it." **George Foreman**

"I'm more interested in what I discover, than what I invent." **Paul Simon**

"I've had a lot of worries in my life, most of which never happened." **Mark Twain**

"If have seen further, it is by standing on the shoulders of giants" **Isaac Newton**

"If you are not having fun, you are doing something wrong." **Groucho Marx**

"If you see a great master, you will always find that he used what was good in his predecessors - and that it was this which made him great." **Goethe**

"In three words I can sum up everything I've learned about life: It goes on." **Robert Frost**

"It can be very frustrating, offering advice. That's because it is rarely welcomed - especially by those who need it the most." **Andy Owen**

"It gets harder the more you know. Because the more you find out, the uglier everything seems." **Frank Zappa**

"It is not the strongest of the species that survive, nor the most intelligent, but the one most responsive to change." **Charles Darwin**

"It is not what we do, but also what we do not do, for which we are accountable." **Moliere**

"It's a funny thing about life. If you refuse to accept anything but the best, you very often get it." **Somerset Maugham**

"Just be nice, take genuine interest in the people you meet, and keep in touch with people you like. This will create a group of people who are invested in helping you because they know you and appreciate you." **Guy Kawasaki**

"Knowledge is power." **Francis Bacon**

"Life can only be understood backwards; but it must be lived forwards." **Søren Kierkegaard**

"Life is 10% what happens to us and 90% how we react to it." **Charles R. Swindoll**

"Life is not measured by the number of breaths we take, but by the moments that take our breath away." **Maya Angelou**

"Life is what happens, while you're busy making other plans." **John Lennon**

"Life isn't about waiting for the storm to pass - it's learning how to dance in the rain." **Vivian Greene**

"Most of the problems in life are because of two reasons: we act without thinking or we keep thinking without acting." **Zig Ziglar**

"No one cares how much you know, until they know how much you care." **Franklin D. Roosevelt**

"Not how long, but how well you have lived, is the main thing." **Seneca**

"Only a life lived for others is a life worthwhile." **Albert Einstein**

"People are smart. They have built-in bullshit detectors. They can reason. They can sense deception and hyperbole." **George Tannenbaum**

"Save your money. You're going to need twice as much money in your old age as you think." **Michael Caine**

"Some men see things as they are and say, why? I dream of things that never were and say, why not?" **George Bernard Shaw**

"Style is knowing who you are, what you want to say - and not giving a damn." **Orson Welles**

"Take it easy. Don't let the sound of your own wheels make you crazy." **Jackson Browne**

"Tell me and I'll forget; show me and I may remember; involve me and I'll understand." **Xun Kuang**

"The farther backward you can look, the farther forward you are likely to see." **Winston Churchill**

"The greatest challenge to any thinker is stating the problem in a way that will allow a solution." **Bertrand Russell**

"The greatest enemy of knowledge is not ignorance; it is the illusion of knowledge." **Stephen Hawking**

"The mariner to sail with is he who has been shipwrecked. For he knows where the reefs are." **Daniel Defoe**

"The more I read, the more I acquire, the more certain I am that I know nothing." **Voltaire**

"The only limit to our realization of tomorrow will be our doubts of today." **Franklin D. Roosevelt**

"The only true wisdom is knowing you know nothing." **Socrates**

"The thing is to try to do as much as you can in the time that you have." **Kenneth More**

"The unexamined life is not worth living." **Socrates**

"There are four groups of people in the world. 1. Those who make things happen. They are the smallest group. 2. Those who watch things happen. They are the next smallest group. Those who don't know what's happening. They are the largest group. Those who don't care if things happen or not. They are known as 'The Pathetic Apathetic." **Andrew Goh**

"There are places I'll remember all my life, though some have changed. Some forever, not for better, some have gone and some remain." **John Lennon**

"There are two motives to action - self-interest and fear." **Napoleon Bonaparte**

"We are what we repeatedly do. Excellence, then, is not an act, but a habit." **Aristotle**

"Walk away. From jobs, from people, from enticements, if they try to nickel-and-dime you or otherwise sully your resolve. My therapist of two centuries taught me a sentence and I stick to it: "I'm sure you can find someone to do what you want, at the price you're willing to pay." That's all. No good relationship, business or personal, starts with a negotiation." **George Tannenbaum**

"We are interested in others when they are interested in us." **Publius Syrus**

"We may lose and we may win, but we will never be here again." **Jackson Browne**

"We measure our days out in steps of uncertainty not turning to see how far we've come. And peer down the highway from here to eternity and reach out for love on the run." **Al Stewart**

"Wisdom begins in wonder." **Socrates**

"What's happening now is what happened before - and often what's going to happen again sometime or other." **Orson Welles**

"When you have eliminated the impossible, whatever remains, however improbable, must be the truth." **Sherlock Holmes**

"Whenever in doubt, turn off your mind, relax - and float downstream." **John Lennon**

"Wisdom cannot be imparted. Wisdom that a wise man attempts to impart always sounds like foolishness to someone else. Knowledge can be communicated, but not wisdom." **Hermann Hesse**

"Wisdom is not a product of schooling but of the lifelong attempt to acquire it." **Albert Einstein**

"You need great passion, because everything you do with great pleasure, you do well." **Juan Manuel Fangio**

"The world is changed by your example, not by your opinion." **Paulo Coelho**

"My philosophy is it's none of my business what people say of me and think of me. I am what I am, and I do what I do. I expect nothing and accept everything. And it makes life so much easier." **Anthony Hopkins**

"We old hippies wear our hair long, because we were part of something that meant more to us than ego and income." **Robert Plant**

"Excellence is not a skill, it's an attitude." **Ralph Marston**

"You can't always get what you want. But if you try sometimes, well, you might find you get what you need." **Mick & Keith**

"You're as young as you feel. As young as you want to be. There's an old saying I heard from a friend of mine. People ask him, "Why do you look so good at your age?" He'll say, "Because I never let the old man in." And there's truth to that. It's in your mind, how far you let him come in." **Clint Eastwood**

"I was sixty years old. I still had to make a living. I looked at my social security check of $105 and decided to use that to try to franchise my chicken recipe. Folks had always liked my chicken." **Colonel Sanders**

"Fear of what other people will think, is the single most paralysing dynamic in business and in life. The best moment of my life was the day I realised that I no longer give a damn what anybody thinks. That's enormously liberating and freeing - and it's the only way to live your life and do your business." **Cindy Gallop**

"When you reach the top, that's when the climb begins." **Michael Caine**

"What's meant to be, will always find a way." **Trisha Yearwood**

"Where's the fire, what's the hurry about? You better cool it off before you burn it out. You got so much to do and only so many hours in a day. But you know that when the truth is told, you can get what you want or you can just get old." **Billy Joel**

Humour and Perspective

'Let's face it, we all need a good laugh now and again.

The world's a bad old place these days and seemingly getting worse by the day.

And, what's more, loads of people take themselves much too seriously – so, a good chuckle regularly, is essential to put everything into perspective.

This section is a celebration of wit, offering a lighter look at life's complexities. It's a reminder that humour is not just the best medicine - it's also a brilliant way to illuminate truth and wisdom.'

"A day without laughter is a day wasted." **Charlie Chaplin**

"A synonym is a word you use when you can't spell the word you first thought of." **Burt Bacharach**

"Age is something that doesn't matter, unless you are a cheese." **Luis Buñuel**

"Always borrow money from a pessimist. He won't expect it back." **Oscar Wilde**

"No pleasure is worth giving up, for the sake of two more years in a geriatric home in Weston-Super-Mare." **Kingsley Amis**

"Direct marketing probably began, when an advocate of the world's oldest profession solicited her first customer. As her business grew, she hired somebody to make the solicitations for her, and that person founded the first direct marketing agency." **Al Eicoff**

"Do not take life too seriously. You will never get out of it alive." **Elbert Hubbard**

"Doing business without advertising is like winking at a girl in the dark. You know what you are doing, but nobody else does." **Stuart Henderson Britt**

"Every morning in Africa, a gazelle wakes up. It knows that it must outrun the fastest lion, or it will be killed. Every morning in Africa, a lion wakes up. It knows that it must run faster than the slowest gazelle, or it will starve to death." **Ray Jutkins**

"Every morning in Marketing Land, a load of dumb marketers wake up. They couldn't give a shit either way." **Andy Owen**

"Everybody's got to believe in something. I believe I'll have another beer." **W.C. Fields**

"Everything is funny, as long as it's happening to somebody else." **Will Rogers**

"Humour is perhaps a sense of intellectual perspective: an awareness that some things are really important, others not; and that the two kinds are most oddly jumbled in everyday affairs." **Christopher Morley**

"I am not afraid of death; I just don't want to be there when it happens." **Woody Allen**

"I am so clever that sometimes I don't understand a single word of what I am saying." **Oscar Wilde**

"I do not fear death. I had been dead for billions and billions of years before I was born and had not suffered the slightest inconvenience from it." **Mark Twain**

"I feel sorry for people who don't drink. When they wake up in the morning, that's as good as they're going to feel all day." **Dean Martin**

"If we were meant to talk more than listen, we would have two mouths and one ear." **Mark Twain**

"If you could kick the person in the pants responsible for most of your trouble, you wouldn't sit for a month." **Theodore Roosevelt**

"If you think you are too small to make a difference, try sleeping with a mosquito." **Dalai Lama**

"If you want to tell people the truth, make them laugh, otherwise they'll kill you." **Oscar Wilde**

"It was just a few short years ago that the 'voice' hype machine was promising us 'voice' was going to be the next marketing miracle that was going to "change everything." Sadly, like so much marketing tech horseshit that was going to change everything (blockchain, 3-D printing, NFTs, self-driving cars, drone delivery, 5G, crypto, virtual reality and, God help us, the metaverse), 'voice' has turned out to be mostly hot air from marketing cretins to whom every new gimmick becomes an obsession. Alexa has turned out to be the world's most expensive way to get a weather report." **Bob Hoffman**

"Just remember, once you're over the hill, you begin to pick up speed." **Arthur Schopenhauer**

"Life does not cease to be funny when people die, any more than it ceases to be serious when people laugh." **George Bernard Shaw**

"Life is like a sewer - what you get out of it depends on what you put into it." **Tom Lehrer**

"Life is too important to be taken seriously." **Oscar Wilde**

"Life is too short to be living somebody else's dream." **Hugh Hefner**

"Nothing is yours permanently, so you'd better enjoy it while it's happening." **Joan Rivers**

"Pay little heed to talk about America becoming illiterate. First off, today's illiterates aren't your market (unless you sell reading courses). Second, if cockroaches, fruitcakes, and opera can survive, so will the written word." **Bill Jayme**

"Some age, others mature." **Sean Connery**

"Someday, someone will break you so badly that you will become unbreakable." **The Joker**

"The brain is a remarkable organism. It starts work the moment you wake up in the morning and doesn't stop until you get into the office." **Robert Frost**

"The business philosophy of Daley Enterprises is simple, but effective. You make contact with your customer and understand their needs. And then you flog them something they could well do without." **Arthur Daley**

"The key to success is sincerity. If you can fake that, you've got it made." **George Burns**

"The longer I live, the more convinced am I that this planet is used by other planets as a lunatic asylum." **George Bernard Shaw**

"The older I get, the more I admire and crave competence, just simple competence, in any field from adultery to zoology." **H.L. Mencken**

"The secret of success? 1. I got up early. 2. I worked hard. 3. My father struck oil." **John Paul Getty**

"When life gives you lemons, squirt someone in the eye." **Cathy Guisewite**

"Whenever anything happens anywhere, somebody over 50 signs the bill for it." **P.J O'Rourke**

"You know, Wall Street is the only place people ride to in a Rolls-Royce, to get advice from people who take the subway." **Warren Buffet**

"Correct capitalisation is the difference between helping your Uncle Jack off a horse - and helping your uncle jack off a horse." **Andy Owen**

"I can resist everything except temptation." **Oscar Wilde**

"Definition of rock journalism: People who can't write, doing interviews with people who can't think, in order to prepare articles for people who can't read." **Frank Zappa**

"If you can't annoy somebody, there is little point in writing." **Kingsley Amis**

"Don't wait until your deathbed to tell people how you feel. Tell them to fuck off now." **Ian Dewar**

Critical Views and Commentary

'I've always believed in calling a spade a shovel.

Tell it the way it is, I say. If they don't like it, then tough titty.

Don't get me wrong, I'm not rebellious for the sake of it. But if something's not right, I will voice an opinion, not sit on my hands with my mouth zipped shut.

Life is too short to endure nonsense. It has to be called out in my book.

This section is a platform for wonderfully provocative thoughts and bold commentary on the issues shaping our world. It's about sparking debate, encouraging reflection - and daring to see things differently.'

> "A committee is a cul-de-sac down which ideas are lured and then quietly strangled." **Sir Barnett Cocks**
>
> "Another flaw in the human character, is that everybody wants to build and nobody wants to do maintenance." **Kurt Vonnegut**
>
> "Anyone who expects fairness in this life, is seriously misinformed." **Jack Higgins**
>
> "Be awfully nice to 'em goin' up, because you're gonna meet 'em all comin' down." **Jimmy Durante**
>
> "Criticism may not be agreeable, but it is necessary." **Winston Churchill**
>
> "Critics are men who watch a battle from a high place then come down and shoot the survivors." **Ernest Hemingway**
>
> "Data is an expense. "Knowledge is a bargain." **Lester Wunderman**
>
> "Doubt is not a pleasant condition, but certainty is absurd." **Voltaire**
>
> "Happiness in intelligent people is the rarest thing I know." **Ernest Hemingway**

"How many times can a man turn his head and pretend that he just doesn't see?" **Bob Dylan**

"I believe the word 'digital' does not need to be used at all. I find 'digital' a tiresome word." **Jeremy Bullmore**

"I can hire men to do everything but two things – think and do things in the order of their importance." **Henry Doherty**

"I cannot think of another trade that has such a need for talent." **Jeremy Bullmore**

"I like to listen. I have learned a great deal from listening carefully. Most people never listen." **Ernest Hemingway**

"I sat watching TV one night and saw 3 bad ads in a row - and I just thought, isn't it amazing how so many clever people sit around a table, with so much money involved - and it takes so long, yet so much of what comes out of the creative process is so mediocre?" **Gillian Rightford**

"I used to practice piano for hours - and now, with a synthesizer, you can input the music and the machine perfects the song. That's why we have so many people in the music business who should be plumbers. They don't really understand music because they haven't been trained." **Quincy Jones**

"I would rather deal with a tyrant any day than a committee. Committees, as a general rule, aren't willing to take chances, which is why you have a committee in the first place - so you can share the blame." **Hal Riney**

"If everyone is thinking alike, then somebody isn't thinking." **George S. Patton**

"If you don't know where you're going, any road will take you there." **Lewis Carroll**

"Ignorance is the root cause of all difficulties." **Plato**

"If you listen to many of the most influential current marketing leaders, it seems that books and studying in marketing are out, completely out. Training is not essential for marketing success. It's appropriate around now for those who don't have any formal training in marketing to start getting defensive about why not being trained is entirely acceptable. While they expect their accountants, dentists, undertakers and engineers to be fully trained, the marketing Philistines make a small exception when it comes to marketing, which is 'creative' and 'common sense'. It's neither of these two things." **Mark Ritson**

"If your company has a clean-desk policy, the company is nuts and you're nuts to stay there." **Tom Peters**

"I'm just flabbergasted at the dumbness of the people I come across - account executives who are even more useless than they were in my day - copywriters with the loosest grasp of the English language. Two of the most dangerous people I've ever come across, now have senior lecturing jobs at Kingston University. I really despair. To be honest, I'm glad I've left the business." **Roger Millington**

"In my experience, committees can criticize, but they cannot create. Search the parks in all your cities - you'll find no statues of committees." **David Ogilvy**

"In the septic tank that is the ad industry, digital advertising is the stuff flopping around at the bottom. Advertising has always been 99% crap, but online advertising has set a new standard of awfulness." **Bob Hoffman**

"It hurts me to write this but advertising is now a form of pollution. Seriously, the collapse of the advertising market could be the best thing to happen to advertising in decades. It could give it back to people who care about people." **Patrick Collister**

"It is the mark of an educated mind to be able to entertain a thought without accepting it." **Aristotle**

"It turns out that people over 42 (*i.e.,* Gen X, Boomers, and Golden Oldies) have 93.5% of the wealth in the US. Gen Z and Millennials, the only groups the idiotic marketing industry pays any attention to, have a combined 6.5% share of wealth. And what do our geniuses in the marketing industry do? They devote a whopping 5 to 10% of their marketing dollars to people over 50." **Bob Hoffman**

"It's the weirdest paradox, that as advertising has drifted to the margins of British cultural life, its sense of its own importance and sense that it has the right to tell people what to do, has increased exponentially." **Steve Harrison**

"Let me tell you something about these big corporation, shit-talking, flat-tire CMOs. They love to pontificate about their bullshit "communities" and their bullshit 'opt-in' experiences, but *they don't dare rely on them.* If they didn't have hundreds of millions to spend on advertising to propel their businesses, they'd all be driving for Uber." **Bob Hoffman**

"Nothing great can come from more than three people in a room." **George Lois**

"Question everything. Learn something. Answer nothing." **Euripides**

"Religion is like a blind man looking in a black room for a black cat that isn't there - and finding it." **Oscar Wilde**

"That euphoria that you get when you pitch for - and win - a new client, is the start of a downhill spiral." **Andy Owen**

"The absence of probity and maturity that Facebook has displayed, has been baked into the company's DNA by Zuckerberg's arrogance - and will remain there as long as his vapid philosophies define their culture. '*Young people are just smarter*'. '*Move fast and break things.* This is the credo of an infantile egotist. You can draw a straight line from this nonsense to the current headlines." **Bob Hoffman**

"The best time to plant a tree was 20 years ago. The second-best time is now." **Chinese Proverb**

"The best way to predict the future is to invent it." **Alan Kay**

"The only thing more frustrating than slanderers, is those foolish enough to listen to them." **Chris Jammi**

"The only thing necessary for the triumph of evil is for good men to do nothing." **Edmund Burke**

"The only thing worse than being blind, is having sight but no vision." **Helen Keller**

"The opinion of 10,000 men is of no value, if none of them know anything about the subject." **Marcus Aurelius**

"The problem is not people being uneducated. The problem is that people are educated just enough to believe what they have been taught, but not educated enough to question what they have been taught." **Richard Feynman**

"The stupidity of marketing professionals seems to be increasing even faster than global temperatures." **George Tannenbaum**

"The waste involved in using mass media, to reach even smaller markets is reaching truly extraordinary proportions. The cost of advertising paid for and never seen, or that is squandered on an audience that includes fewer than one out of ten real prospects, is a recurring nightmare for ad managers." **Stan Rapp**

"The whole problem with the world is that fools and fanatics are always so certain of themselves - and wiser people so full of doubts." **Bertrand Russell**

"Those who fail to study the lessons of history are condemned to repeat them." **George Santayana**

"The ad industry is now the least trusted industry in the world." **Bob Hoffman**

"There is no one in the world with a functioning brain who doesn't understand that the tracking-based adtech industry is a criminal racket of epic proportions. It is a giant worldwide scam - organized crime on a global scale, involving virtually every major corporation, pretty sounding trade organizations and the entire advertising, marketing and online media industries." **Bob Hoffman**

"There is no pain, you are receding, a distant ship, smoke on the horizon. You are only coming through in waves, your lips move but I can't hear what you're saying. I have become comfortably numb." **Roger Waters**

"To avoid criticism, do nothing, say nothing, be nothing." **Elbert Hubbard**

"To criticize is to volunteer." **Audrey Hepburn**

"To live is the rarest thing in the world. Most people exist, that is all." **Oscar Wilde**

"In the end, this world will go under because of the stupidity of people." **George Harrison**

"To paraphrase *The Declaration of Independence* – 'All men and women are created equal. All deserve to be treated equally and be given equal opportunities.' Noble words - but if you're treating your *most* valuable customers the same way you treat your *least* valuable customers, you may be making a mistake." **Alan Rosenspan**

"We are all in the gutter, but some of us are looking at the stars." **Oscar Wilde**

"We are supposed to deeply listen. That's the reason behind our disdain for advertising these days, no one listens." **George Tannenbaum**

"We can easily forgive a child who is afraid of the dark; the real tragedy of life is when men are afraid of the light." **Plato**

"We do not see things as they are, we see them as we are." **Anaïs Nin**

"We've got to fight every day to keep mediocrity at bay." **Van Morrison**

"Why does it matter that you can track who likes a Tweet? You don't track customers as they walk through a supermarket, inspecting products, picking them up and putting them back on the shelf. So, why waste your time tracking useless digital data? After all, knowing someone has visited your website is not essential to business success. Neither is knowing someone liked or shared a social post. If you focus on the marketing basics, you'll get a better return on your time, not to mention your bottom line. And you'll probably be able to grow your budget by removing the marketing clerks who just push pixels and count the points for very little result." **Malcolm Auld**

"You cannot get an A if you're afraid of getting an F." **Quincy Jones**

"You are as young as your faith – as old as your doubts. As young as your self-confidence – as old as your fears. As young as your hope – as old as your despair. Years may wrinkle the skin, but to give up enthusiasm wrinkles the soul." **Samuel Ullman, 19th century Rabbi & scholar**

"Is advertising worth saving? From an economic point of view, I don't think that most of it is. From an aesthetic point of view, I'm damn sure it's not; it is thoughtless, boring and there is simply too much of it." **Howard Gossage**

"To look at a thing, is very different from seeing it." **Oscar Wilde**

"Never get paid once for doing something twice." **Jerry Weintraub**

Inspirational & Motivational

'The heartbeat of every dream is the drive to achieve it.

This final section is a burst of inspiration, a push to take that leap of faith. Harnessing the power of believing in ourselves, overcoming obstacles and pursuing our passions with relentless determination.

I have been moved to source and compile this wonderful mosaic of human experience and wisdom, delivered by true legends – which will inspire, challenge and uplift us all.'

"Act as if what you do makes a difference. It does." **William James**

"Actions speak louder than meetings." **Lee Clow**

"And, in the end, the love you take, is equal to the love you make." **Paul McCartney**

"And it's whispered that soon, if we all call the tune, then the piper will lead us to reason." **Robert Plant**

"Be yourself; everyone else is already taken." **Oscar Wilde**

"Believe in yourself. You are braver than you think, more talented than you know - and capable of more than you imagine." **Roy T. Bennett**

"Everything you've ever wanted is on the other side of fear." **George Addair**

"Do what you can, with what you have, where you are." **Theodore Roosevelt**

"Dream as if you'll live forever, live as if you'll die today." **James Dean**

"Believe you can and you're halfway there." **Theodore Roosevelt**

"Dream big and dare to fail." **Norman Vaughan**

"I could give you a fish, which would feed you for one day. Or I could teach you how to fish, which would feed you for the rest of your life." **Lao-Tzu**

"I want to be thoroughly used up when I die, for the harder I work, the more I live. I rejoice in life for its own sake." **George Bernard Shaw**

"If a thing is worth doing, it is worth doing well. If it is worth having, it is worth waiting for. If it is worth attaining, it is worth fighting for. If it is worth experiencing, it is worth putting aside time for." **Oscar Wilde**

"If we all did the things we are capable of, we would astound ourselves." **Thomas Edison**

"If you can dream it, you can do it." **Walt Disney**

"It is during our darkest moments that we must focus to see the light." **Aristotle Onassis**

"It is only when we take chances, when our lives improve. The initial and the most difficult risk that we need to take is to become honest." **Walter Anderson**

"It is the struggle itself that is most important. We must strive to be more than we are. It does not matter that we will not reach our ultimate goal. The effort itself yields its own reward." **Gene Roddenberry**

"Keep your eyes on the stars, and your feet on the ground." **Theodore Roosevelt**

"Keep your face always toward the sunshine - and the shadows will fall behind you." **Walt Whitman**

"Life has become immeasurably better since I have been forced to stop taking it seriously." **Hunter S. Thompson**

Words That Move Mountains

"Life is short. Break the rules. Forgive quickly, Kiss slowly. Love truly. Laugh uncontrollably - and never regret *anything* that makes you smile." **Mark Twain**

"Make the mind run the body. Never let the body tell the mind what to do. The body will always give up." **George S. Patton**

"My dear friend, clear your mind of can't." **Samuel Johnson**

"My philosophy is just ten words. Each has only two letters. Memorise them - then do them. *If it is to be, it is up to me.*" **Sid Friedman, America's top salesman**

"No man was ever wise by chance." **Lucius Annaeus Seneca**

"No one can make you feel inferior without your consent." **Eleanor Roosevelt**

"Nothing comes from nothing. You must continuously feed the inner beast that sparks and inspires." **George Lois**

"Passion is contagious." **Gary Vaynerchuk**

"Pessimism leads to weakness, optimism to power." **William James**

"Positive thinking is more than just a tagline. It changes the way we behave." **Harvey Mackay**

"Pricing is the exchange rate you put on all the tangible and intangible aspects of your business. Value for cash." **Patrick Campbell**

"Someone's sitting in the shade today because someone planted a tree a long time ago." **Warren Buffett**

"Sunrise doesn't last all morning; a cloudburst doesn't last all day. All things must pass." **George Harrison**

"The best and most beautiful things in the world cannot be seen or even touched - they must be felt with the heart." **Helen Keller**

"The best way to cheer yourself, is to try to cheer someone else up." **Mark Twain**

"The one thing that's common to all successful people: they make a habit of doing things that unsuccessful people don't like to do." **Michael Phelps**

"The only way to do great work, is to love what you do." **Steve Jobs**

"The point today is the point every day. Don't be everyone else. Don't dress like everyone else. Don't think like everyone else. Don't create like everyone else. Don't speak like everyone else. Be *you*. And no one else." **George Tannenbaum**

"The world doesn't owe you anything. It was here first." **Mark Twain**

"Pour your heart and soul into your business. People will notice" **Gary Vaynerchuk**

"There is very little difference between one man and another; but what little there is, is very important." **William James**

"We are stardust, we are golden - and we've got to get ourselves back to the garden." **Joni Mitchell**

"To be yourself in a world that is constantly trying to make you something else, is the greatest accomplishment." **Ralph Waldo Emerson**

"We don't stop playing because we grow old; we grow old because we stop playing." **George Bernard Shaw**

"We're born alone, we live alone, we die alone. Only through our love and friendship can we create the illusion for the moment, that we're not alone." **Orson Welles**

"What lies behind us and what lies before us are tiny matters compared to what lies within us." **Ralph Waldo Emerson**

"What you get by achieving your goals is not as important as what you become by achieving your goals." **Zig Ziglar**

"Whatever you might hope to find, among the thoughts that crowd your mind, there won't be many that ever really matter." **Jackson Browne**

"You have enemies? Good. That means you've stood up for something, sometime in your life." **Winston Churchill**

"You have power over your mind – not outside events. Realize this, and you will find strength." **Marcus Aurelius**

"You have your way. I have my way. As for the right way, the correct way - and the only way - it does not exist." **Friedrich Nietzsche**

"You miss 100% of the shots you don't take." **Wayne Gretzky**

"You must be the change you wish to see in the world." **Mahatma Gandhi**

"Think of things not as they are, but as they might be. Don't merely dream - but create." **Robert Collier**

"Your time is limited, don't waste it living someone else's life." **Steve Jobs**

"It is no use saying, 'We are doing our best.' You have got to *succeed* in doing what is necessary." **Winston Churchill**

"And still, after all this time, the sun never says to the earth, *'You owe me.'* Look what happens with a love like that - it lights the whole sky." **Hafiz**

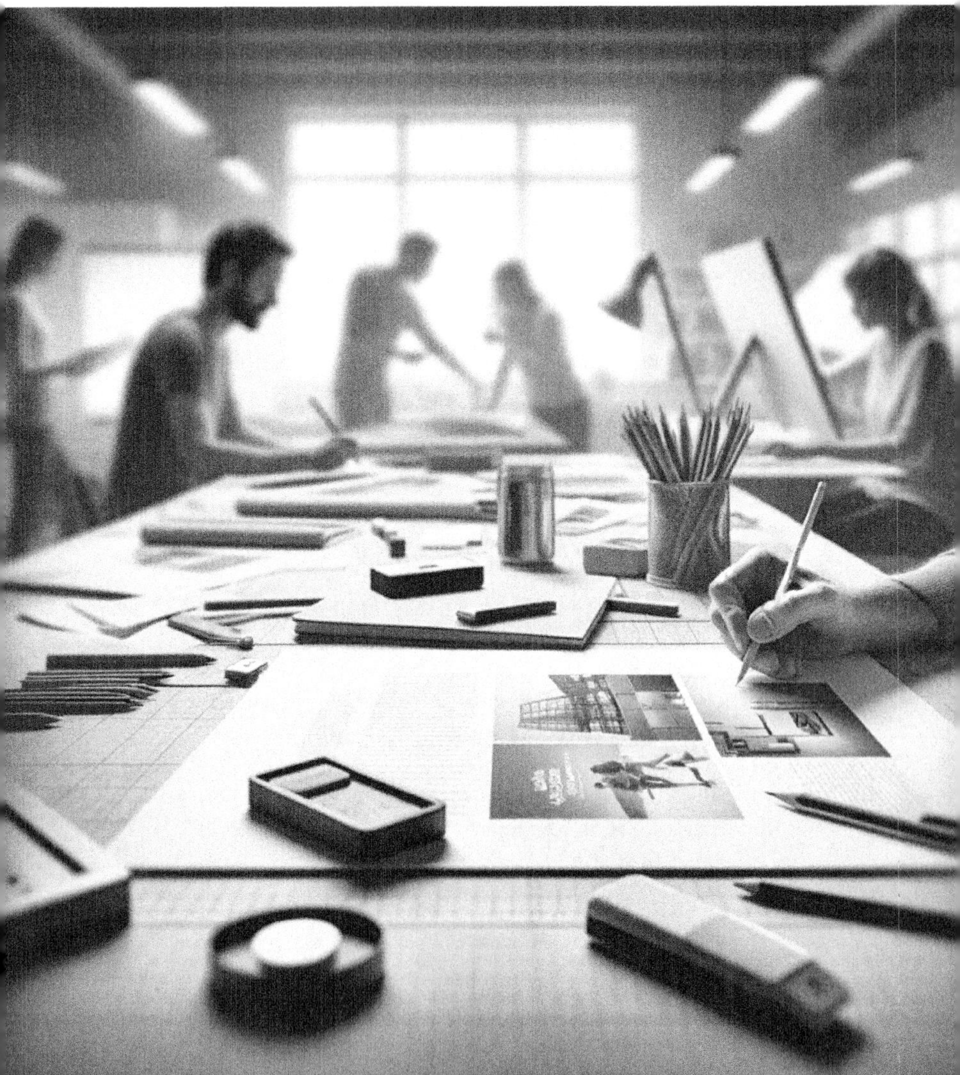

SECTION 2 - CREATIVE

As we know, creativity is a journey that can be both hugely rewarding and massively disappointing in equal measure.

Anyone working with creativity will have experienced both. And, of course, will almost certainly experience them again.

Imagination, vision, knowledge and experience are a rare mix, but when they do come together, the results can be extraordinary, reminding us that true creativity transcends the ordinary to make a meaningful mark on the world.

This section will provide you with insights from the industry's most brilliant minds - individuals who have been there and done it - many times, against all the odds.

There are 8 sections within this category. They are:

The Essence of Creativity

Creativity vs. Effectiveness

The Creative Process

Challenges to Creativity

Creativity and the Consumer

Creativity and Innovation in Advertising

Creativity Under Scrutiny

Personal Insights on Creativity

You will discover the delicate balance between innovation and effectiveness, the challenges to creative freedom - and the profound impact of our work on the consumer's heart and mind.

Be prepared to be inspired to think differently - and to rediscover the spark that drives groundbreaking ideas.

The Essence of Creativity

'Let me take you down, 'cos I'm going to…

…a world where creativity isn't just about being different; it's about making a difference.

These quotes explore what lies at the very heart of creative thinking in marketing, advertising and communication.

It's not about the next big thing, but about simply making things better.

I've gathered many great thoughts that remind us why creativity is so crucial and how it transcends mere novelty, to breathe life, soul and relevance into the creative challenges we face.'

> "All this talk of creativity has me worried. I fear lest in seeking the creativity, we lose the sell." **Bill Bernbach**

> "Big ideas come from the unconscious. This is true in art, in science and in advertising. But your unconscious has to be well informed, or your idea will be irrelevant. Stuff your conscious mind with information, then unhook your rational thought process. You can help this process by going for a long walk, or taking a hot bath, or drinking half a pint of claret." **David Ogilvy**

> "Creativity has much to do with experience, observation and imagination - and if any one of those key elements is missing, it doesn't work." **Bob Dylan**

> "Creativity involves breaking out of expected patterns in order to look at things in a different way." **Edward de Bono**

> "Creativity is contagious, pass it on." **Albert Einstein**

> "Creativity is more than just being different. Anybody can plan weird; that's easy. What's hard, is to be as simple as Bach." **Charles Mingus**

> "Creativity is seeing what everyone else has seen - and thinking what no one else has thought." **Albert Szent-Györgyi**

"Creativity may well be the last legal unfair competitive advantage." **Howard Gossage**

"Creativity requires the courage to let go of certainties." **Erich Fromm**

"Creativity thrives on a consistent diet of challenges and opportunities." **Lee Clow**

"I have never made the slightest effort to compose anything original in my life." **Mozart**

"Make it simple. Make it memorable. Make it inviting to look at. Make it fun to read." **Leo Burnett**

"Nothing is new except arrangement." **Will Durant**

"All art is theft." **Picasso**

"Search the world - and steal the best." **Murray Raphel**

"Promise a lot, but deliver more." **Rosser Reeves**

"Promise, large promise, is the soul of an advertisement." **Samuel Johnson**

"Protect & Serve is the motto of most police departments around the world. It should also be true of your marketing." **Alan Rosenspan**

"Reach out and touch your marketplace. Let them know you care. Be personal. Communicate. And do it often." **Ray Jutkins**

"Talent hits a target no one else can hit; Genius hits a target no one else can see." **Arthur Schopenhauer**

"The secret is finding something that you offer, that's better or different than anything your competitors can offer. When you find it, that is your superstar. Put everything you have behind it and sell it like crazy." **Andy Owen**

"The basis of every great advertisement is a credible promise." **Kurt Vonnegut**

"The creative adult is the child who survived." **Ursula K. Le Guin**

"The verbal and visual elements of an ad, should be as indivisible as the words and music of a song." **George Lois**

"There are rarely new ideas. Just new ways of interpreting the old ones. Originality is often nothing more than a pair of fresh eyes." **Murray Raphel**

Creativity vs. Effectiveness

'It's a delicate dance, balancing the need for genuine creativity with the vital importance of effectiveness.

Not many people know how to do it.

I have brought together the views and thoughts of many, to demonstrate how true creativity doesn't just mean it catches your eye - but it also captures your heart and convinces your mind.

These insights reveal the art of ensuring our brightest ideas not only let us rise above the tripe, but also enable us to connect, engage and sell, proving that the most brilliant creative thoughts are those that can often lead to life-changing triumphs.'

"Advertising is salesmanship. It is not fine art. It is not literature. It is not entertainment." **David Ogilvy**

"Every single element in an advertisement - headline, subhead, photo and copy - must be put there not because it looks good, not because it sounds good, but because testing has shown that it works best!" **John Caples**

"Every promotional message should do 2 things: Encourage a response and enhance the brand." **Andy Owen**

"Every type of advertiser has the same problem; namely, to be believed. The mail-order man knows nothing so potent for this purpose as the testimonial, yet the general advertiser seldom uses it." **James Webb Young**

"Getting attention is not parallel to offering a benefit." **Herschell Gordon Lewis**

"Good advertising says to people, 'Here's what we've got. Here's what it will do for you. Here's how to get it'." **Leo Burnett**

"It is better to be looked over than overlooked." **Mae West**

"I keep on beating the drum for advertising that sells and flogging those who think that advertising is entertainment. I will go to my grave believing that advertisers want results and that the advertising business may go to its grave believing otherwise." **David Ogilvy**

"It's a matter of timing. Selling is like seduction." **Gary Halbert**

"Reach and frequency is essential. It builds awareness, which can lead to interest, which can turn into a sale." **Ray Jutkins**

"Solution is woefully over-used nowadays. Do not tell me your proposition offers a solution without also telling me the following - precisely what my problem is and precisely how your deal will solve it." **John Hancock**

"The amount of effort put into optimising the efficiency - and even the effectiveness - of targeting, relative to the amount of effort that's put into optimising the creative approach, is totally out of whack." **Rory Sutherland**

"The fact is, 'creativity', whatever that is, has almost nothing to do with effective advertising." **Jim Rosenfield**

"If you set out to win awards, you won't have a snowball in hell's chance of doing something that works. And, oh yes, you'll be out of a job in six months." **Steve Harrison**

"What makes your product so unique, different and special? What's in it for your customers that they can't get anywhere else? Not answering those questions will deter clients and impede sales." **Michel Fortin**

"In the modern world of business, it is useless to be a creative original thinker unless you can also sell what you create." **David Ogilvy**

"Effective advertising is a believable promise to the right audience." **John Caples**

"Without a sense of urgency, desire loses its value." **Jim Rohn**

"Advertising is fundamentally persuasion - and persuasion happens to not be a science, but an art." **Bill Bernbach**

"Don't think. Thinking is the enemy of creativity. It's self-conscious, and anything self-conscious is lousy. You can't try to do things. You simply must do things." **Ray Bradbury**

"A good ad has something I call 'calm density.' It's packed with facts, with information, ideas. You can't get that without doing a lot of research." **Gene Schwartz**

The Creative Process

'This is an opportunity to wander into the secret garden of creativity, which is a showcase of ideas, developed from the seeds of knowledge, experience, success, failure and an open mind.

It's not an easy place to find. Many look for it for years and never find it.

These quotes from inspirational people, help to unravel the secrets of the vital journey, from how an idea is born, to the development and delivery of it - the knowledge generated from it - and the on-going journey to continually get better.'

"A designer knows he has achieved perfection not when there is nothing left to add, but when there is nothing left to take away." **Antoine de Saint Exupéry**

"A mind is like a parachute. It doesn't work if it is not open." **Frank Zappa**

"An essential aspect of creativity is not being afraid to fail." **Edwin Land**

"An idea can turn to dust or magic, depending on the talent that rubs against it." **Bill Bernbach**

"An idea is nothing more, nor less, than a new combination of old elements." **James Webb Young**

"Curiosity about life in all of its aspects, I think, is still the secret of great creative people." **Leo Burnett**

"Direct can rebuild what advertising has squandered, because it's one-to-one, it's real people talking to real people - and it's personal." **Patrick Collister**

"Fortune favours the prepared mind." **Louis Pasteur**

"How difficult it is to be simple." **Vincent Van Gogh**

"How you gather, manage, and use information will determine whether you win or lose." **Bill Gates**

"If people knew how hard I worked to get my mastery, it wouldn't seem so wonderful at all." **Michelangelo**

"In every work of genius, we recognize our once rejected thoughts." **Ralph Waldo Emerson**

"Once you replace negative thoughts with positive ones, you'll start having positive results." **Willie Nelson**

"Shakespeare was more original than his originals. He breathed upon dead bodies and brought them to life." **Walter Savage Lando**

"Take David Ogilvy's great Rolls Royce ad. David will tell you that he took the campaign almost completely out of 3 pages of Hopkins' Scientific Advertising, written nearly 40 years before. The Rolls Royce campaign was described in detail – how it should be written, what it should say." **Rosser Reeves**

"The 5 fundamentals for writing a good advertisement: 1. Get attention. 2. Show people an advantage 3. Prove it 4. Persuade people to grasp this advantage 5. Ask for action." **Victor Schwab**

"The heart of creativity is discipline." **Bill Bernbach**

"The mark of highest originality, lies in the ability to develop a familiar idea so fruitfully, that it would seem no one else would ever have discovered so much to be hidden in it." **Johann Wolfgang Goethe**

"Advertising should talk to one person at a time." **Draper Daniels**

Challenges to Creativity

'Creativity faces many challenges – lack of knowledge about what works and what doesn't, committee consensus, lack of client bravery, recipient apathy - and many, many other things.

Here, I shine a light on these challenges with advice and observations from creative giants who have endured them and found the courage to break through them.

These perspectives shared, are beacons for navigating through the fog, guiding us to keep our creative spirit unchained, our beliefs strong and intact - and our innovative flame burning bright.'

"A good advertisement is one which sells the product without drawing attention to itself." **David Ogilvy**

"As most ad and marketing geeks do, I made the mistake of forgetting that advertising is of little to no consequence to most people." **Bob Hoffman**

"Do not fear mistakes - there are none." **Miles Davis**

"I am an advertising man. And I long for the day when it will become a business for a grown man." **Howard Gossage**

"Like I always say, the marketing industry can complicate the shit out of a salami sandwich." **Bob Hoffman**

"Probably the single biggest challenge to creative excellence in communication campaigns, is client stupidity and laziness. They leave everything to the last minute, cannot write a meaningful brief to save their lives - and then expect the very finest copy and creative solutions in a ridiculously short space of time. If you want top quality work, respect the artist and give the artist time to deliver the magic." **Andy Owen**

"Living a life having your worked judged by the Philistines of the world is scary. Screw 'em." **George Lois**

"Marketers are a strange lot. They actively ignore the lessons of history rather than learn from them." **Malcolm Auld**

"Marketers do not know where their digital advertising is appearing, who they are paying, or what they are getting." **Bob Hoffman**

"No one wants to have a relationship with your brand. They might consider an affair for a short while, but it will be on their terms. Believe it, because it's true." **Andy Owen**

"Nothing that's forced can ever be right, if it doesn't come naturally, leave it." **Al Stewart**

"Onwards and upwards and never give your failures a second thought." **George Lois**

"What you do speaks so loudly that I cannot hear what you say." **Ralph Waldo Emerson**

"It pays to promise a benefit which is unique and competitive and the product must deliver the benefit you promise. Most advertising promises nothing. It is doomed to fail in the marketplace." **David Ogilvy**

"Advertising is a genuinely troubled industry with a questionable future. Ad agencies have evolved backwards. What's common today is to hear someone ask: 'What do they mean by that?' Or: 'What is that commercial about?' I think the industry has almost totally abdicated the notion of making a connection with the consumer." **Ed McCabe**

"Time pressure stifles creativity, because people can't deeply engage with the problem. Creativity requires an incubation period." **Steve Harrison**

"This is a peculiar time. Never before has creativity been more valuable – yet felt less valued." **Rory Sutherland**

"If you want creative workers, give them enough time to play." **John Cleese**

"I am certain AI has massive implications for the future. But I am equally certain that human stuff - you know, the 'I' without the 'A', is still the ultimate expression of so many things. In marketing our almost instantaneous obsession with AI, signals (once again) our love for the pornography of change and our fundamental ignorance that our discipline is founded on empathy for the other, for the consumer. And I believe the human instrument remains the best one to understand, communicate and create for other humans." **Mark Ritson**

"We have to continually be jumping off cliffs and developing our wings on the way down." **Kurt Vonnegut**

Creativity and the Consumer

'Creativity that doesn't sell, is failed creativity.

It's all about the targeted recipients of the message. If the creative approach doesn't touch them, make them sit up, take notice and respond positively, then it has been a waste of time and money.

These quotes give us strong, proven advice – and cover how to craft creative efforts to touch, resonate, engage and move the people we aim to reach.'

"Art is not what you see, but what you make others see." **Edgar Degas**

"Consumer interaction with Banner ads is 8 in 10,000. Those figures make 'online conversations' about brands a fantasy." **Bob Hoffman**

"Good advertising is written from one person to another. When it is aimed at millions, it rarely moves anyone." **Fairfax Cone**

"Good direct marketing not only influences and persuades people to act, it also affects the way they think and feel. It *can* and *does* build brands." **Bill Jayme**

"Human beings are the laziest species on the planet – we always seek the path of least resistance. One of the key reasons apps are so popular for example, is their ease of use. So, marketers have to make it as easy as possible for people to buy – which is why giving punters incentives, offers, propositions and reasons to 'buy now' are key to getting sales." **Malcolm Auld**

"I think we've forgotten how to reach people other than award judges and chief creative officers." **George Tannenbaum**

"If you spend your advertising budget entertaining the consumer, you are a bloody fool." **David Ogilvy**

"In direct mail, the letter *sells*, the brochure *tells*." **Andy Owen**

"It is far, far easier to sell more to the customer you have, than it is to sell to a new customer." **Murray Raphel**

"It takes a big idea to attract the attention of consumers and get them to buy your product." **David Ogilvy**

"I've learned that people will forget what you said, people will forget what you did, but people will never forget how you made them feel." **Maya Angelou**

"Maintain your frequency, because you will soon be forgotten." **Murray Raphel**

"Men's natures are alike; it is their habits that divide them." **Confucius**

"Most sales are lost because the salesman presented his product before he knew what motivated his prospect." **Harry Browne**

"Nothing is so powerful as an insight into human nature." **Bill Bernbach**

"Our job is to get noticed. To move people. To motivate people to act and remember." **George Tannenbaum**

"People only buy for two reasons - Solutions to Problems or Good Feelings." **Murray Raphel**

"Remember that the reader's attention is yours for only a single instant." **John Caples**

"Stopping advertising to save money is like stopping your watch to save time." **Henry Ford**

"The envelope is a sales person who must make a good first impression. You never have a second chance to make a good first impression." **Siegfried Vogele**

"The majority of campaigns fail to give consumers enough information." **David Ogilvy**

"There are 4 main reasons why people will notice and respond to an advertising or marketing message: 1. The product has relevance and attraction to them. 2. The product is inherently different. 3. The promotional message is unusual. 4. It is a message that they keep on seeing." **Winston Fletcher**

"When executing advertising, it's best to think of yourself as an uninvited guest in the living room of a prospect who has the magical power to make you disappear instantly." **John O'Toole**

"Words do the selling. Not pretty pictures. The right words and proven copy techniques are absolutely essential to get inside the minds of our targets and influence them to do the positive things we want them to do - like respond and buy." **Andy Owen**

"Don't make ads simple because you think people are low in intelligence. Some are smart and some are not smart. The point is, that people are thinking about other things when they see your ad. Your ad does not get their full attention or intelligence. Your ad only gets a fraction of their intelligence. People won't study your ad carefully. They can't be bothered. And so, you have to make your ads simple." **John Caples**

"Your brand is a story unfolding across all customer touch points." **Jonah Sachs**

"When someone has read your ad, they want to know what to do. Tell them." **John Caples**

Creativity and Innovation in Advertising

'This is where we celebrate the sparks that ignite change - those original thoughts that become milestones.

Campaigns that rise above. Campaigns that deliver extraordinary results.

These quotes showcase how creativity meets innovation, transforming advertising into something that doesn't just demand our attention but captivates our imagination as well.

They highlight the quality of the pioneers whose daring ideas have left indelible marks on our minds and hearts.'

"A gifted product is mightier than a gifted pen. No matter how skilful you are, you can't invent a product advantage that doesn't exist." **Gary Bencivenga**

"Advertising is propaganda; marketing is exploitation." **Howard Gossage**

"Advertising should be news. If it is not news, it is worthless." **Adolph S. Ochs**

"Don't ever let some half-assed marketer's idea of purpose, empathy, empowerment - or whatever happens to be the brand babbler cliché of the month - get in the way of a great idea." **Bob Hoffman**

"If it doesn't sell, it isn't creative." **David Ogilvy**

"If you find you have two potential ways to move forward with your communications strategy and you're undecided which way you should go - choose the bolder option." **Andy Owen**

"If you're not failing now and again, it's a sign you're not doing anything innovative." **Woody Allen**

"In advertising, not to be different is virtually suicidal." **Bill Bernbach**

"Originality: the most dangerous word in the advertiser's lexicon." **Rosser Reeves**

"Sell people what they want to buy! So obvious, so overlooked, and so important." **Gary Halbert**

"The aim of marketing is to get more people to buy more stuff, more often, at higher prices, so the company makes more money." **Sergio Zyman**

"The attention-value of an advertisement is approximately twice as important as the actual convincingness of the test itself." **Daniel Starch**

"The purpose of art is to stop time." **Bob Dylan**

"The greatest thing you have working for you, is not the photo you take, or the picture you paint; it's the imagination of the consumer. They have no budget, they have no time limit - and if you can get into that space, your ad can run all day." **Don Draper**

Creativity Under Scrutiny

'This section looks very closely at what we consider to be effective creative. We all, of course, have different views and thoughts on this.

But one thing is very clear. Standards have slipped badly in the last few decades. Very badly. And those standards continue to head south.

This section feels that pain and calls for a creative renaissance, a necessary move towards authenticity and genuine innovation, using knowledge that has been gained.

Let's question, critique and demand more from our creative endeavours, striving for a standard that respects the past and uses it to forge an improved and more meaningful future.'

> "85% of all advertising today, is invisible, because it is so badly done. 14% of all advertising is very poor - either ugly, stupid, patronising or demeaning. The remaining 1% is terrific advertising." All of us working in this industry, should be bloody ashamed of that." **Andy Owen**

> "Advertising as an industry has always been morbidly preoccupied with its own 'image', largely, I think, because it has little notion of its real identity." **Howard Gossage**

> "Advertising touches everyone in the land - which is why everyone knows more about it than you." **Jeremy Bullmore**

> "Consumers are annoyingly impervious to understanding the finer points of product positioning, differentiation and brand meaning." **Bob Hoffman**

> "I don't know you. I don't know your company. I don't know your company's product. I don't know what your company stands for. I don't know your company's customers. I don't know your company's record. I don't know your company's reputation. Now, what was it you wanted to sell me?" **Gilbert Morris**

"I think we could say that the creativity of an idea works in inverse proportion to the amount of time available and the number of people involved." **Howard Gossage**

"It would appear that there is a theory in certain circles, that if you want to influence millions of very ordinary C2DE people to become interested and purchase your products, you must fill your commercial with very ordinary C2DE looking people. This flawed approach is based on the belief that those watching will then make a connection with the situation. They will see that the product is used by very ordinary C2DE persons very like themselves and will go out and purchase it immediately. Poppycock." **Jeremy Bullmore**

"Young creative people start out hungry. They're off the street; they know how people think. And their work is great. Then they get successful. They make more and more money, spend their time in restaurants they never dreamed of, fly back and forth between New York and Los Angeles. Pretty soon, the real world isn't people. It's just a bunch of lights off the right side of the plane. You have to stay in touch if you're going to write advertising that works." **Jerry Della Femina**

"If you aim at nothing, you will hit it every time." **Zig Ziglar**

"It's a sad fact, but if you read just one book a year during the course of your career, you'll be among the top five per cent most learned people in the industry. Indeed, you could probably claim guru status." **Steve Harrison**

"Every really good creative person in advertising has always had two noticeable characteristics. First, there was no subject he could not easily get interested in. Second, he was an extensive browser in all sorts of fields of information." **James Webb Young**

"Advertising isn't brain surgery. People live and think in broad strokes. Ask some guy in a mall about cars. He'll tell you Volvos are safe; Porsches are fast and Jeeps are rugged. Boom! Where's the rocket science here? There isn't any. You want people who feel X about your product to feel Y. That's about it. We're talking one adjective here. Most of the time, we're talking about going into the customer's brain and tacking one adjective onto a client's brand. That's all. De Walt tools are tough. Apple Computers are easy to use" **George Lois**

"Competitions are for horses, not artists." **Bela Bartok**

"Ninety-nine percent of advertising doesn't sell much of anything." **David Ogilvy**

Personal Insights on Creativity

Join the visionaries in our field, drawing from their deep wells of wisdom.

You can learn so much from these great people. These personal stories and reflections offer guidance for your own creative quest, shedding light on the path to discovering your unique voice and vision.

It's about embracing failure, celebrating curiosity - and the relentless pursuit of creative excellence.'

> "I can't remember ever seeing a really outstanding ad that couldn't be traced to an outstanding ego." **Howard Gossage**

> "In a survey by Epsilon and Phronesis Partners among over 250 digital marketers about the expected demise of 3rd party cookies, they found that 70% of digital marketers believe that by eliminating 3rd party cookies, the industry is '*headed in the wrong direction*'." **Bob Hoffman**

> "In the main, an awful lot of marketing people around these days, appear to have so little depth of experience and knowledge of anything - and are not well read." **Andy Owen**

> "Is advertising worth saving? Yes, if we can learn to look at advertising not as a means for filling so much space and time but as a technique for solving problems." **Howard Gossage**

> "It seems to me that sites like LinkedIn and Facebook have constructed advertising rules specifically so that advertisers create ads that are almost wholly ineffective." **George Tannenbaum**

> "It's impossible to have a conversation with a marketing geek without having to listen to a stream of verbal diarrhea about the metaverse." **Bob Hoffman**

> "Over the past ten years or so, the business has turned into one I no longer understand." **George Tannenbaum**

> "People build brands the way birds build nests. Through the straws and scraps they chance upon." **Jeremy Bullmore**

"People don't buy from clowns." **Claude Hopkins**

"Programmatic advertisers just take money, throw it up in the air and believe any horseshit they are fed, about where it lands." **Bob Hoffman**

"Sending unsolicited spam through marketing automation tools, under the guise of social selling on LinkedIn, is a disgraceful reflection on our industry – and it needs to stop now." **Malcolm Auld**

"Small leaks sink great ships." **Ben Franklin**

"We must learn to use our imaginations first and our computers second." **Lester Wunderman**

"Good is the enemy of great. And it's true when you think about it. Good is easy to like and makes you its friend and says *'Hey, I'm not so bad, am I?'* And you agree. Next thing that happens, is your campaign is good. And that's bad. Good is no longer good enough for the tough challenge today." **Andy Owen**

"Everyone is born creative; everyone is given a box of crayons in kindergarten. Then when you hit puberty, they take the crayons away and replace them with dry, uninspiring books on algebra, history, etc. Being suddenly hit years later with the 'creative bug' is just a wee voice telling you, *'I'd like my crayons back, please.*" **Hugh MacLeod**

"Have no fear of perfection, you'll never reach it." **Salvador Dalí**

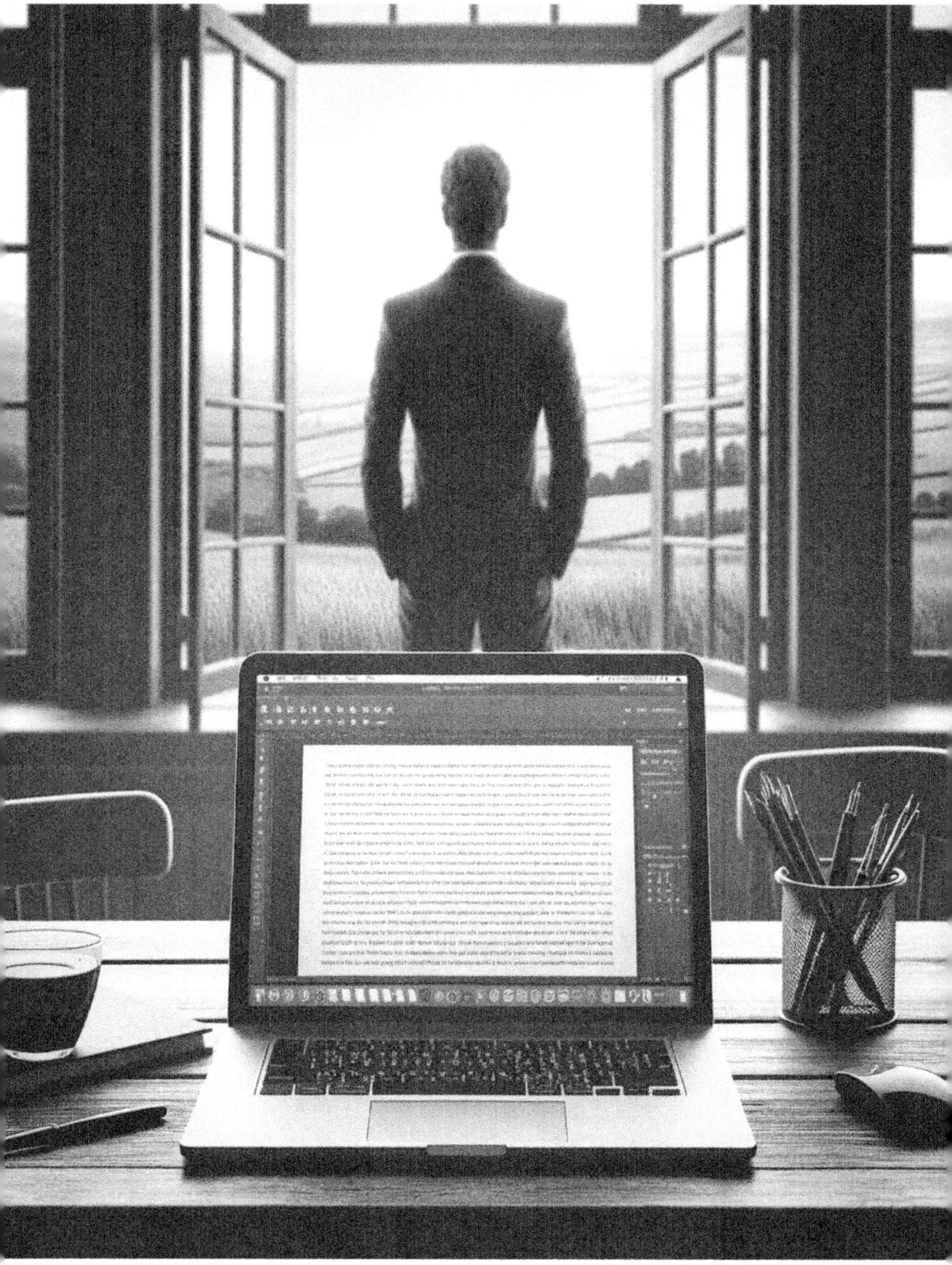

SECTION 3 - COPY

This is my personal *passion*.

I am, first and foremost, a writer. A wordsmith, as it was once called.

I *love* to write.

And I believe in the power of words.

At the core of most of the memorable marketing and advertising campaigns over the passage of time, are the words used.

They made the difference.

They were responsible for the success. Almost without exception.

The reason is simple. Words do the selling - not pretty pictures.

Always *have*. Always *will*.

There are 10 sections within this category, dedicated to the art of writing copy that turns suspects into prospects, prospects into customers, customers into clients and clients into advocates.

The Writing Process

Understanding Your Audience

Crafting Compelling Messages

Creativity and Originality

Headlines and Attention-Grabbing Techniques

Persuasion and Emotional Appeal

Clarity and Simplicity

Testing and Optimisation

Inspirational and Motivational

Ethics and Authenticity

The guidance you will hear, is from the very finest copywriters the world has ever seen - individuals that are masters of their art - and the like of which, we will <u>never</u> see again.

They are here to share their secrets and expertise with you.

You will discover the essentials of understanding your audience, crafting messages that cut through the noise - and the relentless pursuit of perfection in every single word written.

The invaluable insights and priceless advice as to how these legends created narratives that connected, engaged and inspired a positive response, will spark your imagination - and push the boundaries of what's possible.

The Writing Process

'Writing for response is a creative journey. From the shambles of the first draft, to the finished product.

It's a discipline, a devotion - a constant dance of re-imagining and refining.

Finally, after endless edits, the beautiful new baby is born from perseverance, knowledge and the relentless pursuit of perfection.

The true essence of copywriting is forged in the fires of dedication and passion. Please believe it, because it's true.'

> "A campaign should be built around a single overriding selling point, undiluted by a confusion of multiple claims. You cannot chop a tree in two, by hitting it every time in a different place." **Claude Hopkins**

> "A letter should look and feel like a letter." **Dick Benson**

> "Also keep in mind that the more points you try to cover, the less effective each point and therefore your ad, will be. An effective ad will actually only have one central focus, even if you discuss it from two or three perspectives. If your points are too diverse, they compete with each other and end up pulling the reader's attention in separate directions." **James Loftus**

> "As a copywriter, your life will be mercifully easier when you work with great and worthy products, that have a clear-cut, built-in, unique superiority. You'll find your copy often writes itself." **Gary Bencivenga**

> "Broadly speaking, the short words are the best, and the old words best of all." **Samuel Taylor Coleridge**

> "Copy is a direct conversation with the consumer." **Shirley Polykoff**

> "Copy that sells, is copy that is long on hard facts and benefits. Copy is not short or long, it is interesting or uninteresting. It's really as simple as that." **Ray Jutkins**

> "The first draft of anything is shit." **Ernest Hemingway**

"Every product has a unique personality and it is your job to find it." **Joe Sugarman**

"The opening paragraph of a letter or email, is a killing field. So, how can we not only get across it, but also use it as a springboard to propel the reader into the rest of the copy? Firstly, make the sentences short. Make it easy on the brain and easy on the eye. No more than 8 words. 4 is good, 2 can be even better and ONE, on occasions, can be sensational. One other thing - ensure that the promise and interest that you have generated with your envelope copy, letter headline or subject line, is maintained in the opening copy." **Andy Owen**

"Dr Rudolph Flesch's algorithm for good writing is really simple. All you have to remember is: • Short words • Short sentences• Short paragraphs • Active verbs. Seriously, that's it." **John Hancock**

"Every secret of a writer's soul, every experience of his life, every quality of his mind, is written large in his works." **Virginia Woolf**

"Good copywriters take things that no one understands and make them simple and human. Write about them so they become something people will want." **George Tannenbaum**

"Great copy comes from *committed* writers. Writers who study their art *with a passion*. Writers who pay *enormous attention to detail*. Writers with *broad minds* not narrow ones." **Andy Owen**

"He that will write well in any tongue, must follow this counsel of Aristotle: to speak as the common people do, to think as wise men do." **Roger Ascham**

"I am a fast writer - and in a sense I am not interested in words. I don't own a Thesaurus; I don't do crosswords and my dictionary has pictures in it. Words, for me, are servants of the argument and on the whole, I like them to be plain, simple and familiar." **David Abbott**

"If language is not correct, then what is said is not what is meant; if what is said is not what is meant, then what ought to be done remains undone." **Confucius**

"If you can't explain something simply, you don't understand it well." **Albert Einstein**

"If you cannot write well, you cannot think well; if you cannot think well, others will do your thinking for you." **Oscar Wilde**

"If you don't have time to read, you don't have the time (or the tools) to write. Simple as that." **Stephen King**

"In order to write about life, first you must live it." **Ernest Hemingway**

"If you want a convincing sales letter, email or webpage, make sure it is written by a specialist and give them enough time to write and review it, before it has to be delivered. Your investment will be rewarded." **Ian Dewar**

"In a very real sense, your body copy is a minefield that must be navigated with the greatest of care: Every word, sentence and paragraph of body copy represents the chance to either intensify your prospect's focus - or to completely lose him." **Clayton Makepeace**

"Most people who write well, read a lot. Reading good writing, will help you more than reading *about* good writing." **Ken Roman**

"It's not what you say, but what is believed. It's not what you mean, but what is understood." **Ed McLean**

"I've always written very tightly - and there's a good reason for that. There's no point in using words that you're not going to apply." **Theodore Sturgeon**

"No creative writer has ever been able to approach the effectiveness of the boardwalk huckster who often sold 50-75% of his entire audience." **Al Eicoff**

"Nothing is so powerful as an insight into human nature - what compulsions drive a man; what instincts dominate his actions. If you know these things about a person, you can touch him at the core of his being." **Bill Bernbach**

"Say what you are going to say. Say it. Say what you said." **Murray Raphel**

"Specific claims increase believability. Do NOT write in your advertising, 'This car gets great gas mileage.' DO write, *'This car gets 41 mpg in the city and 52 mpg on road trips'*." **Gary Halbert**

"The 5 rules of effective writing. Begin strongly: have one theme: use simple language: leave a picture in the reader's mind: end dramatically." **Winston Churchill**

"The most important thing in communication is hearing what isn't said." **Peter Drucker**

"One hour a day, read. Read *everything* in the world except your business. Read junk. Very much junk. Read so that anything that interests you will stick in your memory. Just read, just read, just read. Subscribe to Ladies Home Journal, Cosmopolitan, Vanity Fair. Get all the very low stuff. Low culture makes big money. Got to remember that! There is your audience. There is the language. There are the words that they use." **Gene Schwartz**

"Perhaps the best advice I can give you, is to concentrate hard on the stuff that you most like to read. Read it with what I call hyper-consciousness. By that I mean that you must be aware not only of what is being communicated, but also how the writer is doing it. Then just copy the best. That's how apprentices have mastered difficult crafts since the stone age." **John Hancock**

"The best copywriters are the most tenacious researchers. Like miners, they dig, drill, dynamite and chip until they have carloads of valuable ore." **Gary Bencivenga**

"If your copywriter isn't a sales person, then he or she will be a poor copywriter. Review your copy right now. If it 'tells' more than it 'sells', sack your writer. He or she will be costing you a lot of money. These days, you simply can't afford it." **Andy Owen**

"The copywriter's challenge is simple. The object of the first sentence is to get the reader to read the second. And so on. If the purpose of all the elements in your communication is to get the recipient to read the copy, then what we are talking about is reading the first sentence. If the reader doesn't read your very first sentence, chances are, that he or she won't read the second." **Joe Sugarman**

"If you want to be a writer, you must do two things above all others: read a lot and write a lot." **Stephen King**

"The first thing is to have the attention of the reader. That means to be interesting. The next thing is to stick to the truth, and that means rectifying whatever's wrong in the merchant's business. If the truth isn't tellable, fix it so it is. That's about all there is to it." **John E Powers**

"The only kind of writing is rewriting." **Ernest Hemingway**

"The letter itself is the pen-and-ink embodiment of a sales person who is speaking personally and directly to the prospect on a one-to-one basis." **Denny Hatch**

"Great sales copy, when read aloud, should sound just like a friend talking to you." **Andy Owen**

"The time to begin writing an article is when you have finished it to your satisfaction. By that time, you begin to clearly and logically perceive what it is that you really want to say." **Mark Twain**

"The tone of a good direct mail letter is as direct and personal as the writer's skill can make it. Even though it may go to millions of people, it never orates to a crowd, but rather murmurs into a single ear. It is a message from one letter writer to one letter reader." **Harry Walsh**

"Good copywriting should be invisible. It should take the reader from where they are, to where you want them to be - without them realising it. But that takes great skill. And it takes great knowledge. If you don't have those, find someone who does." **Andy Owen**

"The writer must have a good imagination to begin with, but the imagination has to be muscular, which means it must be exercised in a disciplined way, day in and day out, by writing, failing, succeeding and revising." **Stephen King**

"There is nothing to writing. All you do is sit down at a typewriter and bleed." **Ernest Hemingway**

"A scrupulous writer, in every sentence that he writes, will ask himself at least four questions, thus: 1. What am I trying to say? 2. What words will express it? 3. What image or idiom will make it clearer? 4. Is this image fresh enough to have an effect?" **George Orwell**

"Don't sell the thing. Sell the life that comes after. People don't buy features, perks, bonuses or discounts. They buy a vision." **Sir John Hegarty**

"Never use a metaphor, simile, or other figure of speech which you are used to seeing in print. Never use a long word where a short one will do. If it is possible to cut a word out, always cut it out. Never use the passive where you can use the active. Never use a foreign phrase, a scientific word, or a jargon word if you can think of an everyday English equivalent. Break any of these rules sooner than say anything outright barbarous." **George Orwell**

"It is natural and harmless in English to use a preposition to end a sentence with." **Kingsley Amis**

"Most good copywriters fall into two categories. Poets and killers. Poets see an ad as an end. Killers as a means to an end. If you are both a killer and poet, you get rich." **David Ogilvy**

"That which is written without effort is generally read without interest." **Dr Johnson**

Understanding Your Audience

'To write for response, it is vital to pull together as much knowledge about the person you are writing to, before you craft even the first word of the first sentence.

Only then can you tailor a sales message that has an above average chance of being attractive to them.

The more they feel you understand them and speak their language, the longer they will read your copy.

You need to write copy that will disarm them without them knowing it – allowing your words to connect, reassure, persuade and work effectively.'

> "A writer must know how people read, what are the main sources of reading errors - and what can be done to possibly forestall them." **Rudolf Flesch**

> "Address the people you seek and them only." **Claude Hopkins**

> "To be successful in marketing these days, companies must recognise that whether an audience is a dozen or millions, people do not respond as a target consumer or as profiled sample - but as me and you - and him and her." **Andy Owen**

> "Always talk up to your prospects, not down. When flattered, people almost always rise to the occasion. When insulted, they rise to walk over to the wastebasket." **Bill Jayme**

> "Every copywriter knows what it is to struggle with a copy for hours, for days - fixing it, polishing it, rearranging it. We have all been guilty of leaving the headline until the last and then spending half an hour on it - or perhaps only ten minutes." **John Caples**

> "Human nature is perpetual. In most respects it is the same today as in the time of Caesar. So, the principles of psychology are fixed and enduring." **Claude Hopkins**

> "If you can't turn yourself into your customer, you probably shouldn't be in the ad writing business at all." **Leo Burnett**

"I think central to good writing of advertising, or anything else, is a person who has developed an understanding of people, an insight into them, a sympathy towards them." **George Gribbin**

"If the client changes the copy, I get very angry. This is because I take a lot of trouble writing it. And what I write, I write on purpose." **J Stirling Getschell**

"If you can't communicate the major benefits of your products and services to your customers and prospects in an effective way, they will not buy them. And you will lose your job." **Andy Owen**

"If you talk to a man in a language he understands, that goes to his head. If you talk to him in his language, that goes to his heart." **Nelson Mandela**

"I don't know the rules of grammar. If you're trying to persuade people to do something or buy something, it seems to me that you should use *their* language. The language *they* use every day. The language in which they *think*." **David Ogilvy**

"It took millions of years for man's instincts to develop. It will take millions more for them to even vary. It is fashionable to talk about changing man. A communicator must be concerned with unchanging man. With his obsessive drive to survive, to be admired, to succeed, to love, to take care of his own." **Bill Bernbach**

"Most marketers have not thought deeply enough about what loyalty is, or what produces it." **Victor Ross**

"Don't think of people in the mass. That gives you a blurred view." **Claude Hopkins**

"Our communications do not fall on virgin soil. They are received by seasoned, skeptical, advertising-literate minds. They see you coming a mile off - and they're ready for you. Accept that fact - and you'll write stronger campaigns." **Andy Owen**

"People will engage with what you have written, when they can see themselves in the story you are telling." **Stephen King**

"When your customer retention and loyalty improves, so will your profit." **Murray Raphel**

"The more mature the customer, the more likely that customer will not tolerate mediocrity in communication. Approach them correctly, respect their status and the fact that they are in now very firmly in control. They are incredibly savvy. Don't try to kid them. They *demand* correctness, so give it to them. Spelling mistakes, typos and poor message delivery, are instant death." **Andy Owen**

"Neatness counts. If what you've written looks formidable, messy or sloppy, then your reader braces for an ordeal, before reading a word." **Ken Roman**

"Your job is not to write copy. Your job is to know your visitors, customers and prospects so well, you understand the situation they're in right now, where they'd like to be - and exactly how your solution can and will get them to their ideal self." **Joanna Wiebe**

"You need to write copy that connects to the 'experiential background of the reader'. Introduce as many facts as you can which are likely to come within that experience. When you do that, you will connect immediately. The reader's reaction is likely to be: *Yes, I know that, so it's likely that the other facts are true.*" **Herschell Gordon Lewis**

"Talk little, listen much. So go and get in touch with your people. Don't lose that. Talk to every cab driver you meet. Speak to everyone you can. Be the best listener you have ever met. That is your market talking. You don't have to have great ideas if you can hear great ideas." **Gene Schwartz**

"The best copy matches the prospect's needs, like a Savile Row suit fits a dandy." **Drayton Bird**

"Remember, the people you address are selfish, as we all are. They care nothing about your interests or profit. They seek service for themselves." **Claude Hopkins**

"Something you know about your customer, is much more important than anything you know about your product." **Harvey MacKay**

"The best copywriters are the ones who can get into the mind of the reader and understand their desires and fears." **Joe Sugarman**

"The most basic of all human needs is the need to understand and be understood. The best way to understand people is to listen to them." **Ralph Nichols**

"The most important thing in advertising is to know and understand your audience, which is the first step in persuading them." **Bill Bernbach**

"The perfect advertisement is one of which the reader can say, 'This is for me - and me alone'." **Peter Drucker**

"When someone tells you that long copy outpulls short, that 6×9 envelopes outpull #10s, and that brochures no longer pay for themselves, don't believe a word of it. No one opens up an envelope because it's a 6×9, or reads a letter because it's long. People open what *interests* them. They read what *interests* them. They respond to what *interests* them." **Bill Jayme**

Crafting Compelling Messages

'Here lies advice and guidance into the <u>real</u> art of copywriting.

Delivered by the very best there has ever been. Copywriting legends with levels of skill and expertise that is almost non-existent today.

These giants share their thoughts, to help you understand the power of words and how to use them correctly. How to structure a communication to turn a suspect into a prospect, a prospect into a customer and a client – and finally, into an advocate.

It is, put simply, effective communication. Writing that works.'

"Ads are not written to entertain. When they do, those entertainment seekers are little likely to be the people whom you want. This is one of the greatest advertising faults. Ad writers abandon their part. They forget they are salesmen and try to be performers. Instead of sales, they seek applause." **Claude Hopkins**

"An ad should ideally be like one end of an interesting conversation." **Howard Gossage**

"An emotion-based sales argument will always outsell an intellect-based sales argument. *Always*." **Herschell Gordon Lewis**

"Do not address your readers as though they were gathered together in a stadium. When people read your copy, they are alone. Pretend you are writing to each of them, a letter on behalf of your client." **David Ogilvy**

"Don't tell me how good you make it; tell me how good it makes me feel when I use it." **Leo Burnett**

"Don't tell me the moon is shining; show me the glint of light on broken glass." **Anton Chekhov**

"Everyone accepts the importance of the unique selling proposition. But very few realise that it needs a unique selling talent to deliver it." **Andy Owen**

"Don't underestimate the value of beginning a headline by naming the people you want to reach." **John Caples**

"Express savings in terms of money, not in percentages. The only percentage people really understand, is 50% and even then, you'd better add, Half Off!" **Bill Jayme**

"Go to any length to get it right. Don't even let the smallest thing slide. If it bothers you even a little bit, work on it until it doesn't." **Luke Sullivan**

"Good copy cannot be written with tongue in cheek, written just for a living. You've got to believe in the product." **David Ogilvy**

"Good copywriting comes from spending a lot of time on it. Revising, polishing, and editing it. The best pieces of copy are the ones I have spent a lot of time on." **David Abbott**

"I never write fewer than sixteen headlines for a single advertisement." **David Ogilvy**

"I spend a lot of time fact-finding and I don't start writing until I have too much to say. I don't believe you can write fluent copy if you have to interrupt yourself with research. Dig first, then write." **David Abbott**

"I use the oldest words in the English language. People think I'm an ignorant bastard who doesn't know the ten-dollar words. I know the ten-dollar words. And they don't work in copy." **Ernest Hemingway**

"It's not just what you say that stirs people. It's the way that you say it." **Bill Bernbach**

"Be so good they can't ignore you." **Steve Martin**

"How shall we know good copy? By the goods it is actually known to sell, Mr. Advertiser!" **John E. Kennedy**

"Let's say you are a manufacturer. Your advertising isn't working and sales are going down and everything depends on it. Your future depends on it, your family's future depends on it, other people's families depend on it. Now what do you want out of me? Fine writing? Do you want masterpieces? Or do you want to see the goddam sales curve stop moving down and start moving up?" **Rosser Reeves**

"Letters are things. Not pictures of things." **Eric Gill**

"Nothing works better than a well-written letter. *Nothing.*" **Andy Owen**

"Of all practical advertising media, only direct mail offers a sufficiently large canvas for telling a complex story." **Bill Jayme**

"Start with the prospect instead of the product. Avoid superlatives and brag-and-boast language. Wherever possible, incorporate anecdotes, testimonials, success stories, and other believable elements of human interest." **Don Hauptman**

"The best writing for marketing and sales is the language you use in everyday conversation. The face-to-face communication you have. As easy as reading the newspaper, listening to the late-night television news." **Ray Jutkins**

"The content of the letter is paramount, whereas its style should be invisible. The reader ought to be impressed by your product and not with the way you have crafted the letter. If a prospect gets to the end of your mailing and thinks 'Wow, what a great letter', then you have failed." **Roger Millington**

"The copywriter uses words as tools to persuade and motivate an audience. You persuade your readers that you have something valuable to offer; you motivate them to acquire it for themselves. This is the essence of effective copywriting." **Richard Bayan**

"In contemporary copywriting, technique comes before art." **Andy Owen**

"The most persuasive words in advertising are simply, REASON WHY. Whether you spread your message on TV, the internet or by letter, you must explain the REASON WHY your product is much better. And while you're at it, don't forget that your audience won't believe you, unless you give the REASON WHY what you claim is true." **Gary Bencivenga**

"When there is a gap between one's real and one's declared aims, one turns as it were instinctively to long words and exhausted idioms, like a cuttlefish spurting out ink." **George Orwell**

"The true communication isn't what you say. It's what the recipient takes away." **Tom Monahan**

"Today's digital world needs clear, strong, precise language more than ever before. There is so much bad information floating around out there – so much bad rhetoric trying to sell bad ideas – that true clarity of thought and word has become a powerful weapon for good in the world. If you can learn to use that weapon, you will not only become successful, you will also become a hero." **John Hancock**

"When something is free, say it six ways to Sunday (for example, *'Free gift comes to you with our compliments' 'Gratis' 'On the house'* or *'It's yours to keep as an outright present, without cost or charge - not a penny.'*" **Bill Jayme**

"If you find there are words and phrases you wouldn't say face to face, rewrite them." **Steve Harrison**

"You are presenting a showcase for your product. Just like a store showcase on Fifth Avenue. You want the person to be able to look through the copy like the person is able to look through the glass in the showcase and see the product inside. If that glass becomes dirty, reflective, or calls attention to itself in any way, you have failed. If you want to write a novel, go write a novel. But don't write novel copy." **Gene Schwartz**

"Don't forget the vital importance of effective punctuation. Commas, dashes, colons, underlines, parentheses and others, are all essential weapons for the knowledgeable writer. Good use of punctuation is essential, as it allows the writer to control the pace of the selling delivery. The pros have known this for decades." **Andy Owen**

"Sell, sell, SELL, every word of the way." **Clyde Bedell**

"Words can be like X-rays if you use them properly – they'll go through anything. You read and you're pierced." **Aldous Huxley**

"Any word you have to hunt for in a thesaurus is the wrong word. There are no exceptions to this rule." **Stephen King**

"Most people write badly because they cannot think clearly. The reason they can't think clearly, is that they lack the brains." **H.L Mencken**

"Writers should strike out any third word on principle. You have no idea what vigour it adds to your style." **Mark Twain**

"If it isn't essential, cut it out." **Ken Roman**

"I was asked recently why a company should hire a professional copywriter. My answer was short and simple. *'Because they will write better than you, that's why.'* Everyone uses words, but only the experienced pro knows how to use the right words effectively, to make a communication zing, grab attention and sell." **Andy Owen**

"The purpose of advertising is to sell. That is what the client is paying for and if that goal does not permeate every idea you get, every word you write, every picture you take, you are a phony and you ought to get out of the business." **David Ogilvy**

Creativity and Originality

'The quest for the extraordinary has always been a fascination for many.

I am constantly searching for it - and drawn to those who have already found it.

As these quotes show - to embrace it, the mind must always be open.

Be disciplined. Take what has gone before, learn from it, steal from it and then, if relevant, break some moulds, defy conventions and create something exciting – and hopefully, extraordinary.'

"All great composers of the past spent most of their time studying. Feeling alone won't do the job. A man also needs technique." **George Gershwin**

"Before you put pen to paper, before you ring for your stenographer, decide in your own mind what effect you want to produce on your reader - what feeling you must arouse in him." **Robert Collier**

"Remember that most businesses make real money only on repeat sales. While a good copywriter can make a prospect hopeful enough to try a product, he or she can't make that customer delighted enough to buy it again. Only you and your product can do that." **Clayton Makepeace**

"Don't just gain a response: gain knowledge." **Graeme McCorkell**

"Don't look for meaning in the words. Listen to the silences." **Samuel Beckett**

"Good writing is not a natural gift. You have to learn how to write well." **David Ogilvy**

"How long should a letter be? The best answer to that age-old question is - as long as it has to be." **Denny Hatch**

"I've written many winners with a letter and no brochure, but none with a brochure and no letter." **Harry Walsh**

"The 4 bases of success in contemporary copywriting, are Connectivity, Clarity, Benefit and Verisimilitude." **Herschell Gordon Lewis**

"If you want to think about yourself primarily as a 'writer', you're probably in the wrong business. To make it as a direct response copywriter, you must be – first and foremost – a salesman. Not a single great copywriter I've ever met thought of him – or herself as a writer who sells. Instead, they saw themselves as a 'sales person in print.' It's a crucial distinction." **Clayton Makepeace**

"Rewrite and test ruthlessly. A change of one word can increase response 250%. Sackheim tested his famous ad at least six times before he found the headline and format that worked. Most copy isn't written in one day. You have to write, rewrite, edit, rewrite, test - and test again. Keep asking yourself, 'would I buy this product and have I said everything to make the sale?" **Joe Vitale**

"The difference between the almost right word and the right word is really a large matter - 'tis the difference between the lightning bug and the lightning." **Mark Twain**

"The person hasn't been born yet, who can sit down and dash off a great piece of direct mail copy. It's hard work. There are no shortcuts. Almost without exception, the success of any direct mail letter is in direct ratio to the time spent on its preparation." **Bob Stone**

"The professional copywriter's ability to adapt the tone of a letter or email will make your copy charming. It will give it personality. This is how outstanding writers disarm their prospect in just the same way as a charming individual can disarm someone, he or she is trying to persuade to do something." **Drayton Bird**

"The smartest, most reliable way to get prospects to read your message and respond is not by cranking up the volume on your promise. That just makes it look like a bigger pile of hype. It is by raising the level of your proof, which sets you apart from the hype, deserving of further investigation." **Gary Bencivenga**

"By the time you have perfected any style of writing, you have always outgrown it." **George Orwell**

"The truth isn't the truth until people believe you - and they can't believe you if they don't know what you're saying. And they can't know what you're saying, if they don't listen to you - and they won't listen to you if you're not interesting. And you won't be interesting unless you say things imaginatively, originally, freshly." **Bill Bernbach**

"When it comes down to it, there are only 3 types of writers. *1. Those who write without thinking 2. Those who think while they write 3. Those who think before they write.* There are literally millions of the first two categories, as we all know to our cost. There are but a handful of the third. They are very rare indeed. Those are the ones you want. The reason is simple. The talented and knowledgeable few in that category are the ones that will produce copy that sells. If you write for response, you really want to be like them." **Andy Owen**

"The purpose of a direct response message is to convince the reader, viewer or listener, to perform a positive act as the direct result of having absorbed the message." **Herschell Gordon Lewis**

"The four most important characteristics of a copywriter are indefatigability, clarity, craziness and humility. Indefatigability is essential for the research; clear writing is an essential element of successful writing; craziness comes from the fact that copywriters look at things other people don't see or even recognise; humility means that the customer comes first, the product second, the writing last." **Gene Schwartz**

"The secret of all effective originality in advertising is not the creation of new and tricky words and pictures, but one of putting familiar words and pictures into new relationships." **Leo Burnett**

"Don't have dinosaur views about long copy. It's not about long or short. It's about interesting or uninteresting. If you take two pages to write something that should be on one page - you will lose the reader because you'll be rambling. If you need two pages to do a complete selling job and you cram it on to one page - your layout will be unattractive and won't sell, so you'll lose them as well. If you don't believe me, test it. Then you will see." **Andy Owen**

Headlines and Attention-Grabbing Techniques

'Headlines and strong openers are much more than just words.

They are the neon light shining through the darkness. The throat-grabber. The 'stopper'.

A handful of carefully chosen words, that scream benefit and relevance. A beacon that draws readers in.

These greats show you how it's done. Listen to them, learn and apply.'

"A headline should single out your prospect like a bell boy paging a man in a crowded hotel lobby." **Claude Hopkins**

"Even today you can look through almost any consumer or professional publication and find headlines that possess not a single one of the necessary qualities, such as self-interest, news, or curiosity." **John Caples**

"First, you have to have impact. You need to get attention. Or what's the point? Second, you have to communicate. You have to say your message clearly and emphatically, so people understand. Finally, you have to persuade. You have to tell people, 'What's in it for them'." **Dave Trott**

"If you fail to get your prospects' attention, you'll fail to deliver your benefits and offer. And if you don't deliver your offer and ask for the sale, it's pretty much a slam dunk that you won't get the sale." **Clayton Makepeace**

"If your advertising goes unnoticed, everything else is academic!" **Bill Bernbach**

"Now I spend hours on headlines - days if necessary. And when I get a good headline, I know that my task is nearly finished." **John Caples**

"If people like you, they'll listen to you, but if they trust you, they'll do business with you." **Zig Ziglar**

"The key to writing good headlines - and good copy - is the same as the key to success in conversation. Don't be a bore. Don't talk about yourself unless you have something really interesting to say." **Drayton Bird**

"Anyone who has done any testing at all, would agree that the headline and deck copy and the first few paragraphs of the main sales copy have a greater impact on response than any other part of a sales promotion." **Clayton Makepeace**

"The success of an entire advertisement campaign may stand or fall on what is said in the headlines of the individual advertisements." **John Caples**

"Some of the most tremendous flops amongst letters and advertisements, contain body matter filled with great copy. But the headline was poor and it never got read." **Victor Schwab**

"Headlines - do they work? I think Hillary would have been picking her administration if she had picked better headlines. Trump had *'Build the wall'*, *'Put her in jail'*, *'Drain the swamp'*. She had *'Break the glass ceiling'*." **Steve Harrison**

"Never make your claim bigger than your proof. And always join your claim and your proof at the hip in your headlines, so that you never trumpet one without the other. Surround your claims with stronger, bolder proof and watch your response soar." **Gary Bencivenga**

"Your outer envelope is where your prospect decides whether to stop, look, and listen. It's the come-on – the headline on the ad, the dust jacket on the book, the display window outside the store, the hot pants on the hooker." **Bill Jayme**

"If you have an important point to make, don't try to be subtle or clever. Use a pile driver. Hit the point once. Then come back and hit it again. Then hit it a third time with a tremendous whack." **Winston Churchill**

"Generalities roll off the human understanding like water off a duck. They leave no impression whatever." **Claude Hopkins**

"Specifics sell much better than generalities. When you have something that you are told 'has a success rate of over 30%', change it to 'has a success rate of 31.4%', as this is so specific, it is much more believable." **Andy Owen**

"The headline is the 'ticket on the meat.' Use it to flag down readers who are prospects for the kind of product you are advertising." **David Ogilvy**

"The headlines are critically important. The majority of the public reads little else when deciding whether or not they are interested." **John Caples**

"On the average, five times as many people read the headline as read the body copy. When you have written your headline, you have spent eighty cents out of your dollar." **David Ogilvy**

"Writing effective headlines is a critical skill. The better your headline, the better your odds of beating the averages and getting what you've written, read and acted on, by a larger percentage of people." **Andy Owen**

"What good is all the painstaking work on copy, if the headline isn't right? If the headline doesn't 'stop' people, the copy might just as well be written in Greek." **John Caples**

Persuasion and Emotional Appeal

'The heart of good writing, is an understanding of people, an insight into them, a sympathy towards them.

Knowledgeable, worldly-wise and well-read copywriters, write the best copy.

If you recognise what compulsions drive people, what instincts dominate their actions – your copy can be crafted to effectively connect, convince and convert.

It's about knowledge - and using it to deliver benefits-driven copy, laced with emotional triggers and underpinned with an irresistible offer.'

> "A package that makes a single request for the order in the last paragraph of the letter is like a salesman with a cold, weak handshake. If he's not confident, neither am I." **Bill Christensen**

> "Advertising has got to sell. In writing ads, act as you would, if you met the individual buyer face to face. Don't show off. Don't try to be funny. Don't try to be clever. Don't behave eccentrically. Measure ads by salesman's standards, not by amusement standards." **David Ogilvy**

> "Each advertisement must make a proposition to the consumer. It must be one that the competition cannot - or does not - offer. It must be so strong that it can move the masses to spend millions on your product." **Rosser Reeves**

> "Emotional words outpull intellectual words every single time in selling copy. There is absolutely NO exception." **Andy Owen**

> "It's only words. And words are all I have, to take your heart away." **Brothers Gibb**

> "It is insight into human nature that is the key to the communicator's skill. For whereas the writer is concerned with what he puts into his writings, the communicator is concerned with what the reader gets out of it. He therefore becomes a student of how people read or listen." **Bill Bernbach**

"When the writing is breezy, uncomplicated, and conversational, it also feels more accessible. But when it's cursed by big fat blocks of text and sentences choked with dependent clauses, long paragraphs that are grammatically perfect but dense, readers can get scared off in a hurry." **John Forde**

"For a creative writer, possession of the 'truth' is less important than emotional sincerity." **George Orwell**

"The head certainly can't go along and concur with the heart without some reasons. Now all this process is one of rationalisation. To rationalise is to bring props of reason to support decisions arrived at emotionally. The skilled copywriter attempts to provide the reader of advertising with a basis for rationalisation. In short, the real advertising writer who is after results, makes the reader want something - and then provides what the reader will consider a good excuse for buying it". **Clyde Bedell**

"Written words can also sing." **Ngũgĩ wa Thiong'o**

"Make your offer so great that only a lunatic would refuse to buy." **Claude Hopkins**

"I have never seen a relevant incentive fail to pay for itself." **Victor Ross**

"The offer is the hook. If you have no offer, you have no bait. It is the quickest way to push up your response rate and, be assured, it is infinitely more important than punctuation or grammar." **Roger Millington**

"He who works with his hands is a laborer. He who works with his hands and his head is a craftsman. He who works with his hands and his head and his heart is an artist." **St Francis of Assisi**

Clarity and Simplicity

'In a marketplace polluted with mediocrity, irrelevance and naïve complexity, clarity is vital.

If your message is unclear, people will be confused. And a confused audience will not buy.

These quotes demonstrate how stripping away the clutter and the passenger words, allow the clear message to shine through.

The purity and power of simplicity is a proven way to convey the core message in its most potent form.'

"Advertising in the final analysis should be news. Use phrases that are not too imprecise and very understandable. Do not be too stuffy; remove pompous words and substitute them with plain words. Minimize complicated gimmicks and constructions. If you can't give the data directly and briefly, you must consider writing the copy again." **Jay Abraham**

"Almost any departure from the standard of black serif type on white or light paper, results in some interference to the reader's ability to read and comprehend text." **Geoffrey Heard**

"Be as generous with your offer as you possibly can." **Graeme McCorkell**

"Body type must be set in a serif font if the designer intends it to be read and understood. More than five times as many readers are likely to show good comprehension when a serif font is used, instead of a sans serif font." **Colin Wheildon**

"Don't make the story bigger than the store." **Murray Raphel**

"Executives and managers at every level are prisoners of the notion that a simple style reflects a simple mind. Actually, a simple style is the result of hard work and hard thinking; a muddled style reflects a muddled thinker or a person too dumb or too lazy to organize his thoughts." **William Zinsser**

"Don't use three words where one will do. Your copy needs to be tight, persuasive, and compelling. You have to hold the reader's attention. Your reader is not waiting to hear from you. Quite the opposite, in fact. You are getting in the way. He/she has no time to work through your copy, because he/she has other pressures - the mortgage is due and finances are tight, or a partner has a bite mark on the neck that he/she didn't put there. Your copy has to be as good as it can possibly be. Always." **Andy Owen**

"Facts can be turned into art, if one is artful enough." **Paul Simon**

"Find the simple story in the product, and present it in an articulate and intelligent, persuasive way." **Bill Bernbach**

"Fine words butter no parsnips." **15th century English proverb**

"If you believe that facts persuade (as I do), you'd better learn how to write a list so it doesn't read like a list." **David Abbott**

"In your copy, delete self-absorbed words like 'We,' 'Us,' and 'Ours,' which do not appeal to your reader's self-interest. Your reader wants to know what is in your offer *for him*." **Denny Hatch**

"It is much harder to simplify than to complicate. Only the best minds and best writers can cut through. In short, writing simply and directly only looks easy. It takes skill and work and fair time to compose." **Professor Joseph Kimble**

"Language is the dress of thought." **Dr Johnson**

"Language is wine upon the lips." **Virginia Woolf**

"Make your copy straightforward to read, understand and use. Use easy words; those that are used for everyday." **Bill Bernbach**

"Never promise more than you can deliver; always deliver what you promise." **Ken Roman**

"One day I'll find the right words - and they will be simple." **Jack Kerouac**

"It isn't about storytelling. It's about telling a story well." **Andy Owen**

"No matter how chic sans-serif type looks, <u>never</u> use it for body copy. It's unreadable. So is body copy set in reverse, copy overprinted on art - and all headlines that run sideways." **Bill Jayme**

"Reading is to the mind what exercise is to the body." **Joseph Addison**

"Short words are best and the old words when short are best of all." **Winston Churchill**

"Simplicity is all. Simple logic, simple arguments, simple visual images. If you can't reduce your argument to a few crisp words and phrases, there's something wrong with your argument. There's nothing long-winded about Liberté, Égalité and Fraternité." **Maurice Saatchi**

"Telling the truth about a product demands a product that's worth telling the truth about. Sadly, so many products aren't. So many products don't do anything better. Or anything different. So many don't work quite right. Or don't last. Or simply don't matter." **Bob Levenson**

"The full stop is there for a reason. It helps people understand what you are saying by chopping your text into bite-sized pieces called sentences. Remember, nothing else matters, except meaning." **George Smith**

"The more elaborate our means of communication, the less we communicate." **Joseph Priestley**

"Let things taste the way they are." **Keith Floyd**

"The most valuable of all talents is that of never using two words when one will do." **Thomas Jefferson**

"The truth of it, is that clarity trumps clever. The more straightforward and clear you are, the more effective you're going to be." **Alan Rosenspan**

"Don't try and be subtle or clever - or try to entertain. The objective is to SELL. As Drayton once said to me, 'Your letter is not written as an artistic endeavour. It is written to build your business'." **Andy Owen**

"These concepts should be part of every mailing package: 'new', 'free', 'save', 'guaranteed', 'hurry'. This concept should be part of every sentence: YOU." **Bill Jayme**

"The single most important thing that makes copy work is benefits. The next most important thing is news. (The best copy contains news of benefits). The final thing is to use emotional words." **Andy Owen**

"In writing, I search for believability, simplicity and emotional impact." **Hal David**

"You never have to change anything you got up in the middle of the night to write." **Saul Bellow**

"One should use common words to say uncommon things." **Arthur Schopenhauer**

"Advertising is competitive persuasion - that's the business we're in. But too often you get over-familiar, blokey-copy from brands you haven't even heard of. And it's often inappropriate. What I want to know is: By what degree will my life be better if I buy your product? Or to put it another way: Why should I give you my money?" **Steve Harrison**

Testing and Optimisation

'Testing is not essential - it is much more important than that.

But, despite its importance, it has dropped off the radar for most these days. Very few people test. That's one of the reasons we all have to suffer wall-to-wall crap every day.

Not testing is a massive mistake. If you don't test, how do you know what works best?

Perfection is not a destination, but a journey of discovery, learning and continually getting better, guided by the insights of testing and the knowledge it provides.'

"Allocate 20% of your marketing budget to testing." **Denny Hatch**

"Almost any questions can be answered cheaply, quickly and finally, by a test campaign. And that's the way to answer them - not by arguments around a table." **Claude Hopkins**

"I don't have thoughts, I have tests." **Jay Abraham**

"If you want to dramatically increase your response, dramatically improve your offer." **Axel Andersson**

"Every single word in selling copy is vitally important. Many times in test activity, the change of one word has dramatically increased the response levels of a letter or ad. One of the most famous was the headline of an ad for an automobile repair kit. The original headline was, 'How To Repair Cars'. A new headline was tested against it, with a one-word change, to 'How To Fix Cars.' The ad pulled 20% more sales. Those are serious numbers." **Andy Owen**

"Never stop testing - and your advertising will never stop improving." **David Ogilvy**

"There are only two rules in direct marketing. Rule1: Test everything. Rule 2: Refer to Rule 1." **Richard V Benson**

"Discovering the most effective appeal is often difficult. Often there are many seemingly attractive appeals, yet only one right one. If my advertising department or agency had a year in which to prepare a campaign for my product, I would be perfectly satisfied if they spent 11 months in search of the right appeal and one month – or one week, for that matter – preparing the actual advertisements." **David Ogilvy**

"Testing is absolutely vital. Okay - which of these will bring the greatest response? A subject line for an email, *'Jason, you're going to like this,'* or *'You're going to like this, Jason.'* Same words, just rearranged. 60 % said 'start with the name and that will grab them.' 40% felt, ending with the name, would force them to go into the message itself. Just worthless opinions. You need to test to find out which one will pull the most response. Under battle conditions, one of those two examples pulled 8% better, which is a significant result. It was the one ending with the name. A lot of people would have lost their shirt." **Herschell Gordon-Lewis**

"Testing is not something you do once and forget. Testing is not something you do only when you have a little extra in your budget. Testing has to be an integral part of your marketing strategy. I call it 'The Testing Loop'. 1) Run a test. 2) Analyse the results. 3) Act based on the results. 4) Repeat." **John Caples**

"There are three main reasons, besides ignorance and laziness, why people don't test. All are wrong. First, they suffer from the fond delusion that they can predict the future. They rarely can. Second, they think they don't have time. Third, there isn't enough money. Yet, strangely enough, I find that somehow they always manage to find oceans of time and money to sort the mess out later." **Drayton Bird**

"If you're not testing and you're not in a continuous improvement mode, you're really stepping back. You're not really succeeding."
Alan Rosenspan

"As a result of nearly four decades of testing, I can share some interesting facts on the importance value of the five key elements of a direct mail pack. They are: *The Targeting 50%, The Letter 23%, The Offer 13%, The Timing 9% and The Creative 5%.* As these percentages show, the copy is over 4 times more important than the creative in a direct mail pack. Not an opinion, by the way. Proven – in the trenches." **Andy Owen**

Inspirational and Motivational

'Great people inspire me. Always have.

And they always will.

Learning from giants like these, has constantly been a source of light in the darkness. Their words, like torches, guide, inspire and propel us forward. But only for those who care to listen...

In the world of words, we are eternally students, seekers and dreamers.'

> "A good head and good heart are always a formidable combination. But when you add to that a literate tongue or pen, then you have something very special." **Nelson Mandela**

> "All you have to do is convey the advantage, not create it out of thin air." **Bill Bernbach**

> "Belief is a fabric of personal experiences." **Professor Poffenberger**

> "Confession is good for the soul and for copy too. Bill Bernbach used to say – a small admission gains a large acceptance." **David Abbott**

> "I admire the writing of Tom Wolfe, but I wouldn't say he influenced my style. Likewise, Dickens. But what writers like these can teach you, is commitment and a dogged determination to rewrite, rewrite and rewrite." **Steve Harrison**

> "I always started by writing 'Dear Charlie', like writing to a friend. And then I would say what I had to say - and at the end I would cross out Dear Charlie - and I was all right." **Bob Levenson**

> "If you want to get better at anything, you need to practice. Writing is no different. If you want to write well, you need to write. Every single day. For as long as you can. Good writers love to write." **Andy Owen**

> "No matter what people tell you, words and ideas can change the world." **Robin Williams**

"Most of us are lazy - and copywriters are no exception. Many study little, if at all. They think the key is ingenuity and clever ideas. They put their faith in flair and luck. They 'pick it up' as they go along. That is the chief reason why most copy is so bad." **Drayton Bird**

"Read, read, read. Read everything - trash, classics, good and bad - and see how they do it. Just like a carpenter who works as an apprentice and studies the master. Read! You'll absorb it. Then write. If it's good, you'll find out. If it's not, throw it out of the window." **William Faulkner**

"So much of what we do in advertising - creating an image or impression of a brand, making something memorable so you buy x instead of y, has to do with the power of words. Yet, our industry does everything in its power to deny, disparage and otherwise mitigate the power of words." **George Tannenbaum**

"Speak in such a way that others love to listen to you. Listen in such a way that others love to speak to you." **Zig Ziglar**

"Steep yourself in your subject, work like hell and love, honor, and obey your hunches." **Leo Burnett**

"The art of communication is the language of leadership." **James Humes**

"The best writing is that which goes FROM the heart, TO the heart - from the heart of the writer, to the heart of the reader." **Benjamin Disraeli**

"The more we study, the more we discover our ignorance." **Shelley**

"The pen is mightier than the sword." **Edward Bulwer-Lytton**

"To read with diligence; not to rest satisfied with a light and superficial knowledge, nor quickly to assent to things commonly spoken" **Marcus Aurelius**

"The words we choose to use every day, can have a massive impact on our lives. The right words can bring us success and everything we want in life. The wrong words can - and very often do - bring us poor results and failure. Underestimate the power of words at your peril." **Andy Owen**

"The written word is the strongest source of power in the entire universe." **Gary Halbert**

"If you want to write, if you want to create, you must be the most sublime fool that God ever turned out and sent rambling. You must write every single day of your life. You must read dreadful dumb books and glorious books - and let them wrestle in beautiful fights inside your head, vulgar one moment, brilliant the next. You must lurk in libraries and climb the stacks like ladders to sniff books like perfumes and wear books like hats upon your crazy heads. I wish you a wrestling match with your Creative Muse that will last a lifetime. I wish craziness and foolishness and madness upon you. May you live with hysteria, and out of it make fine stories - science fiction or otherwise. Which finally means, may you be in love every day for the next 20,000 days. And out of that love, remake a world." **Ray Bradbury**

Ethics and Authenticity

'So many lies. So many untruths. So many cons.

These days, it has become an epidemic. Especially online.

Rise above it. Make your choice; integrity and truth, is the only way.

I've always believed in the power of truth as the foundation of trust. I can't sell by lying.

Crafting messages with a core of ethical truth and authentic resonance is not just a practice, but a duty.'

> "Honesty is not only the best policy. It is rare enough nowadays to make you pleasantly conspicuous." **Charles H Brower**

> "The truth sells a million times better than lies." **Drayton Bird**

> "Advertising is a business of words, but advertising agencies are infested with men and women who cannot write. They cannot write advertisements, and they cannot write plans. They are as helpless as deaf mutes on the stage of the Metropolitan Opera." **David Ogilvy**

> "All sorts of outrageous claims are being made by digital agencies in an attempt to lure unsuspecting marketers to their digital lairs. One such claim is that you need specialist digital copywriting skills for the Internet. What a load of old bollocks. There is only one skill you need to write copy for the Internet. It's the skill known as copywriting." **Malcolm Auld**

> "Be sincere. Communicating sincerely can't be faked. The customer will know in a few moments whether they believe what you have written." **Murray Raphel**

> "Check the signature on your letter. If it looks like the handwriting of an eleven-year-old, and you're selling financial, medical, or insurance services, consult your art director." **Bill Jayme**

"Good copywriting skills come from people with well-furnished minds. They're inquisitive. They explore and investigate. They make it their business to find out more. They are avid readers. Of *everything*." **Andy Owen**

"Great writers often make lousy direct response copywriters. Why? Because the writing gets in the way of the sale. Financial publishers aren't looking for great literature. Nobody ever intentionally rolled out three million losing packages just because they were enchanted by the prose!" **Clayton Makepeace**

"Half the people in advertising haven't read a bloody book about copywriting. They think it's something you pick up - like diphtheria." **Drayton Bird**

"Just because a marketing clerk can type doesn't mean they can write. Hire professionals to write your copy, as you damage your brand every time you use amateurs." **Malcolm Auld**

"Lazily-written sales copy is copy that doesn't attempt to tell or sell - and is just a pointer to the website. This is a wasted selling opportunity. The hardest part is getting your customers' attention, through the thousands of messages that are being inflicted on them every day. To just give customers a line and a URL often just isn't good enough." **Steve Harrison**

"Most copy I read, as an ex-boss of mine used to say, is flat as a plate of piss. It sticks to you like dogshit sticks to a lug-soled boot. I'd imagine that much of the copy that's foisted upon us, does more to depress a brand's value than elevate it." **George Tannenbaum**

"I don't despair anymore. There's no point. It's no good despairing over something that's in a hopeless state – and will *nev*er get better. The trend has been set for years – and it's a racing certainty that it will only get worse. No one cares about copy anymore. It isn't important to marketers at all. It's a necessary evil. Something smelly on the bottom of their shoes. When bad copy gets written – by whichever muppet gets the job this month – it *always* gets approved. The reason is simple. The approver has absolutely no idea of what good copy is – and how good copy works. They have never studied the art. They simply don't know. So, it always looks good to them – and therefore gets approved. If it wasn't so serious, it would be funny. The partially-sighted are leading the blind." **Andy Owen**

"Nobody knows how to write a letter any more. Nobody dares be emotional and let emotions hang out. Maybe it's not politically correct to be emotional. But non-emotional letters do not work." **Denny Hatch**

"Not many people/companies have access to good writers. If you do, you have the advertising equivalent of a more powerful engine in a racing car." **George Tannenbaum**

"Modern writing at its worst, does not consist in picking out words for the sake of their meaning and inventing images in order to make the meaning clearer. It consists in gumming together long strips of words which have already been set in order by someone else - and making the results presentable by sheer humbug. The attraction of this way of writing is that it is easy." **George Orwell**

"Not one client in 100 studies what makes good copy. They think they're qualified to judge it simply because they can write and read." **Drayton Bird**

"Our business is infested with idiots who try to impress by using pretentious jargon." **David Ogilvy**

"Personalize indiscriminately at your peril. Do you really want as a customer, some boob who gets turned on by seeing his own name repeated nine times in a single page?" **Bill Jayme**

"The very first thing I tell my new students on the first day of a workshop is that good writing is about telling the truth." **Anne Lamott**

"I'm fed up to the back teeth of having my copy reviewed and commented on, by people who have no idea about how copy works. I spend a lot of time crafting it. I write it that way for a reason. Then I'm told that he doesn't think a sentence should start with 'And', or he doesn't like this word or that word - and would I please make the changes. Drives me nuts - and I have to tell you, I say 'bollocks' much more often than I once did." **Andy Owen**

"The good writers touch life often. The mediocre ones run a quick hand over her. The bad ones rape her and leave her for the flies." **Ray Bradbury**

"The first thing is to have the attention of the reader. That means to be interesting. The next thing is to stick to the truth, and that means rectifying whatever's wrong in the merchant's business. If the truth isn't tellable, fix it so it is. That is about all there is to it." **John E Powers**

"As any experienced marketer knows, one of the casualties of the digital marketing industry has been the quality of marketing communication. The majority of digital marketing messages don't communicate at all, let alone persuade. The reason is simple – the marketing messages are written by typists, not copywriters." **Malcolm Auld**

"The trouble is, that a huge chunk of business owners, salesmen and third-rate marketing managers with a computer, think they can write copy - and the dumber they are, the more prone they are to do so. These idiots don't even know how to use the spell and grammar check tools that are part of their system. And as for using the dictionary and thesaurus to make sure they are choosing the right words, one might as well whistle in the wind." **Ian Dewar**

"How vain it is to sit down to write when you have not stood up to live." **Henry David Thoreau**

"Letter writing is close to becoming a lost art in this day of e-mail, Internet, word processing, cell phones and answering machines. Many people today seldom, if ever, sit down and write actual letters anymore. On those rare occasions when they do try to write a letter, they often find that their letter-writing skills have atrophied." **Charles Osgood**

"David Ogilvy once asked King George's surgeon what makes a good surgeon. The surgeon replied *'A great surgeon knows more than other surgeons'*. It's the same with copywriters. The best ones know more about the value of words and how to use them *effectively*." **Andy Owen**

"You can divide advertising and marketing people into two groups. The amateurs and the professionals. The amateurs are in the majority. They aren't students of communication. They guess. The professionals don't guess, so they don't waste so much of their client's money." **Drayton Bird**

"Never write an advertisement which you wouldn't want your family to read. You wouldn't tell lies to your own wife. Don't tell them to mine." **David Ogilvy**

"You don't find many direct marketing agencies these days. They've become integrated agencies, through-the-line agencies, total communications agencies, or any such combination that their hard-pressed proprietors can think of. Almost everyone, it seems, is desperate to put as much distance as they can between the dull, traditional, boring and grubby business of getting response - and the shining, creative, fun world of looking after brands and images." **John Watson**

"Every one of the great copywriters I have known - and I have known many - had one thing in common. They studied the past. Every bad copywriter - and I have known far more than good - didn't study the past. Most today, imagine if it isn't digital, it's irrelevant." **Drayton Bird**

ABOUT YOUR AUTHOR

Andy Owen's reputation and respect within the world of direct marketing is well documented. His name is synonymous with creativity, effectiveness and a proven mastery of words.

With a career spanning over four and a half decades, Andy has not only witnessed the evolution of direct marketing, but has played an active part in shaping its trajectory. He has shared his knowledge and passion in Masterclasses, Workshops, Seminars and Events in 29 countries to date.

His induction into the Copywriting Hall of Fame - a rare honour shared by only one other copywriter in Europe - underscores his influential status and contributions to the industry.

Andy's creations are distinguished by their clarity, persuasion and ability to engage and influence audiences deeply and effectively. His work, thoughts and advice are all available to view, read and download, on his company website - *www.andyowencopyandcreative.com*

He also is the author of numerous stories and tales covering a wide range of subjects, all on his personal website - *www.glintoflight.com*

His profound love and devotion to the craft of copywriting make Andy's role in compiling *'Words That Move Mountains'* not just an endeavour, but a destiny.

This inspirational book represents the culmination of a lifetime spent in the pursuit of excellence in communication - and it's a personal tribute to the power of words that have the ability to inspire, influence - and indeed - move mountains.

'Words That Move Mountains' is a true testament to Andy's status as a world-class wordsmith and a passionate and devoted guardian of the transformative power of words.

Printed in Great Britain
by Amazon